"I thoroughly enjoyed this book! It was such a fun read ~~us to 'jump out of the well'. Lily's years of bedside n~~ ~~g~~ ~~the world's~~ top hospitals combined with her business successes in China and America, give her book the unique ability to drive nurse entrepreneurs' success. Her insights have opened up my vision to achieve the life I've dreamed of. Her compelling stories will forever change how you view nurses and nursing."

—**Sarah Raden, RN, MSN**

"Compelling. This 'How-To' manual is the key to unlock the special power that only you possess! Lily opens new doors to us with exciting stories, business opportunities, intelligence and actionable steps. She captivates, informs and inspires each of us to achieve our highest and best. It's a treasure for any nurse or nurse-to-be trying to make sense of the ways to personal and professional success. Lily is a transformational leader. Her entrepreneurial attitude is contagious! Success is by choice not by chance, Lily shows the way!"

—**Rachel Cardosa, RN, DNP**

"Simply insightful, unique, winsome and inspiring! Lily doesn't just tell us how, why and what to do—she does it, and shows us to do the same to succeed. She serves as a powerful example of the truth that she shares. I loved all of Lily's personal stories and ancient success wisdom which drew me in from chapter to chapter, I particularly love the Monkey King story! I can't wait to get this book into the hands of my kids and my friends. No one seriously considering a successful career should be without this book!"

—**Anna L. Mitchell-Gervais, RN, BSN**

"This book awakened me to escape from the 'bottom of the well' and into the winning 'Monkey King' growth mindset. Lily's wonderful, practical examples and 'How-To' tools show the road. There is no doubt in my mind that this book will be the GUIDE of many of us on the journey to achieve the respect, autonomy, freedom and prosperity of our hearts' desire. I am so inspired by Lily's passion! Her diligently practical intelligence and inspiring heart-warming personal experiences, like fuel for your fire, and let your light shine!"

—Renee Kramer, RT, Registered Technologist (Radiology)

"I absolutely love this book! It had me laughing, crying, confident and inspired! Lily has an open and engaging writing style which makes for an enjoyable read. The personal anecdotes she relates are very interesting and encouraging, and her tips are simple and practical! This book doesn't just tell us to fearlessly pursue our dreams—it shows us how to do it. It is full of real life experience, conversation openers, ancient success wisdom, creative ideas and encouraging stories, and I just love the Monkey King story!"

—Nora LeBlanc, RN, BSN

"Truly a lively engaging read that is both highly spiritual and immediately practical. Lily understands that success is not just a matter of making large amounts of money. Success springs from self-respect and the ability to do the 'right thing' on each one of our own terms. I love Lily's passion! This book will definitely inspire not only nurses, but also many other health care professionals for years to come!"

—Mary Jo Goethel, Speech Pathologist

"This book presents us exciting and practical business opportunities and wisdom. Lily combines modern nursing knowledge with ancient Chinese success secret to create unique valuable insights! The stories, questions and recapping are very insightful, friendly, accessible and compelling. It builds new bridges to power partnership opportunities for our financial business entrepreneurs everywhere indeed."

—Deborah Koenes, Financial Operating Manager

UNLOCK!

Nurse Entrepreneurs,
Reclaim Your Hidden Power

Lily Huang Carrier RN, MA

ISBN: 978-0-9974149-1-2

For Colin—

who amazes and motivates me each and every day

Contents

Part 1:

MIND GAMES

Chapter One

Bullying, Babies, Bladders, and Burnout: In Other Words, Being a Nurse

You cannot prevent the birds of sadness from passing over your head, but you can prevent their making a nest in your hair.

—Chinese proverb

AS A NURSE, I KNOW what it feels like: increased patient loads, excruciatingly long hours, high-pressure situations, odd shifts, constant changes in technology and health care practices, and demanding—often unrealistic—expectations from patients, families, colleagues, and administration. Nurses tend to be empathic, patient, and professional, but burnout happens to the best of us. In fact, nearly one in five new nurses leave their job within their first year and one in three leave within two years.[1] The hospital turnover rate is 17.2 percent and bedside nurses' turnover rate is 16.4 percent.[2]

You're a compassionate, intelligent, strong nurse with a tremendous capacity to care for others, but when it comes to caring for yourself, you're lost, aren't you? You are not alone if you are feeling like you can't go on. Nurses all around the world struggle with the impossibilities of their daily lives just like you.

The truth is you are not trapped as a nurse—you do not need to get another degree. You have completed your nursing study to become an LPN or RN. You have all the skills required to become a successful entrepreneur.

Wonderful things happened during my nearly three decades of search for the true path to nursing business and life success.

I acquired the essence of the surprising ancient Chinese success secret, and I am excited to share it with you in the rest of the chapters of this book. I believe that it can be the light to direct your thoughts and your way on the journey of reclaiming your respect, freedom, and prosperity.

Burnout is when you feel emotionally, mentally, and physically drained. After years of caring, educating, and providing a "lifeline" for others day in and day out, it feels as if you may have nothing more to give. Nurses tend to experience burnout much more profoundly than others in the health care field, with approximately 40 percent of hospital nurses reporting burnout levels higher than the norm of health care workers.[3] Why is this? It seems that it is because we care so much for others that we experience stress more profoundly. Researchers at the University of Akron found that nurses who are primarily motivated by the desire to help others, rather than enjoyment of work, were more likely to burn out.[4] When we are tugged in so many directions, when all we want to do is care for others, we feel overwhelmed.

Burnout usually happens gradually over time and has many different causes. Sometimes it's a combination of issues: inadequate staffing, unpredictable schedules, long shifts, physical and mental fatigue, excessive noise in the workplace, unrealistically high workloads, time pressure, lack of collegiality among coworkers, and unsupportive— or even unqualified—supervisors. Nurses encounter challenging patients and families, role conflict and confusion, inadequate resources of all types, underuse of their talent, and sometimes a literally toxic work environment with exposure to radiation, chemicals, and pathogens.[5] So much is out of our control, it feels as if we can't do our jobs properly—which of course leads to even more stress.

OVERSCHEDULING, UNDERSTAFFING

Medical facilities are moving toward 12-hour shifts for ease in scheduling, but a 2016 survey conducted by the Hospital Consumer Assessment of Healthcare Providers and Systems notes that the percentage of nurses who report that their burnout increased as their shift lengthened increased.[6] One study found that nurses who work shifts longer than eight or nine hours were two and a half times more likely to experience burnout.[7] Many nurses love these longer shifts, but the majority of studies indicate that over the long haul, these shifts negatively affect the health and well-being of the nurse. Many complain that it takes a full day to recover from a 12-hour night shift saying, "The day after working nights, isn't really a day off,"[8] and further studies indicate that erratic shifts, night shifts, and long shifts all lead to chronic health concerns such as diabetes and obesity[9] as well as mood alterations, cognitive problems, and recurrent illness.[10]

One survey of over 3,000 nurses showed serious concerns over long work hours: excessive fatigue, recovery times from long shifts, fear of making errors on the job, lack of substantial breaks for rest and lunch that make one feel "on" all the time, and even accidents driving home.[11] Furthermore, long shifts have been proven to negatively affect patients. A groundbreaking study in the journal *Health Affairs* looked at 393 nurses over more than 5,300 shifts and found that those who worked shifts that were twelve and a half hours or longer were three times more likely than others to make an error in patient care.[12] And a 2014 study in the *American Journal of Critical Care* found that nurses who were fatigued, lost sleep, or couldn't recover between shifts were much more likely to regret a medical decision they had made.[13] It certainly can be convenient to work longer shifts, but when one considers the loss of free time due to recovery, the toll it takes on one's health, and the negative effects on patients, it is not worth it.

And, because of the nursing shortage, ineffective management, and staff illness call-ins (more on that later), we are often very understaffed, and the nurse-to-patient ratios are often dangerously low. I remember one shift in cardiac critical care when I was assigned four patients—double the recommended patient-nurse ratio. I know I'm not alone. One veteran pediatric oncology nurse, Martha Kuhl, says that her patient load has consistently doubled over the past thirty-four years. She remembers one night shift when she was the only nurse on duty with five patients: "These are all babies that can't breathe. I felt okay at four," but that last overload patient "sort of tipped it over the edge where I felt unsafe in being able to handle all of these patients."[14] One pediatric nurse, Beth Ann Schwamberger quit her job for similar reasons: "Most nights on the job, I felt unable to provide my patients the high-quality care that they deserved because of being short-staffed and having access to under-trained residents as our primary point of contact," she said. She reported that during one night shift, a patient failed to get a required diagnostic test, and another patient was not placed in intensive care due to a lack of space.[15] One nurse put it this way: "It's not like being a waiter, where you have too many tables, which is stressful, but no one's going to die if they don't get their entree in time."[16] Being overworked and feeling helpless to adequately take care of patients' needs can take its toll.

Not only does understaffing lead to increased stress on nurses, it has an incredibly negative effect on patients. A 2011 study from the University of California finds that lower nurse staffing levels were associated with more deaths, higher failure-to-rescue incidents, higher rates of infection, and longer hospital stays.[17] And another study from 2013 indicated that higher patient loads lead to increased patient readmission rates.[18] What works for hospital management is not working for the nursing staff—and certainly isn't working for nurses or patients—which leads to even more stress and burnout!

BULLYING EACH OTHER?

Besides the stress of understaffing and long hours, there is the issue of a lack of collegiality in the workplace. Research over the past few decades indicates that in increasingly corporate health care environments bullying, or horizontal violence, is a major problem in peer-to-peer relationships between nurses. Many of us use phrases such as "eating their young" to describe the relational dynamics that typify nursing culture. In a 2012 survey of 227 nurses a whopping 77 percent reported that they had witnessed horizontal bullying and 53 percent had experienced it themselves![19] One study from 2015[20] reported the most common bullying behaviors among nurses to be the following:

- Being ignored or excluded
- Having rumors spread about you
- Being ordered to carry out work below your competence level
- Having your professional opinion ignored
- Being given impossible targets or deadlines
- Being allocated an unmanageable workload
- Being humiliated or ridiculed about your work

The article also included several other bullying behaviors, such as repeatedly checking an individual's work, giving someone the silent treatment, belittling, criticizing, scapegoating, sabotaging, and blaming the individual for things that are not within his or her control.[21] Trying to be an effective nurse when colleagues *seem to be working against you*, certainly doesn't help with the stress load.

UNSUPPORTIVE ENVIRONMENT

I have found that the administration and supervisors are genuinely concerned about the overall quality of patient care and are committed to creating a healthy work environment, but some of them are woefully lacking in conflict resolution skills and a fundamental understanding of how to accommodate a staff's concerns. While I was working as a surgical nurse at a large hospital, and after learning that I was pregnant, I requested from my administrators that I did not want to work in—or around— radiology for the remaining months of my pregnancy. They flat-out denied my requests. Sure, they weren't legally obligated to accommodate me, and maybe I was being overly cautious, but I was frustrated that I had absolutely no say over this situation—one that deeply concerned me.

There are many dangerous scenarios in a health care environment. Besides exposure to radiation, nurses face blood-borne pathogens, violent patients and families, communicable diseases, muscle strain, chemical hazards, and even terrorism. We certainly have a right to be concerned. And sometimes we have minor issues, such as light or noise problems, lack of teamwork, staffing problems, communication breakdowns, and lack of resources. When we approach our administration, we want to be listened to and appropriately accommodated. One survey of nearly 8,000 female health care workers found that the "number-one driver for feeling better about their work–life blend was their supervisor."[22] These female health care workers "look to the supervisor to care about them as people, to understand their child care and elder care responsibilities, and to work with them to accommodate those needs."[23] In one survey of stressed-out nurses, one respondent lamented about the major concern with her administration: "Lesser educated/experienced people in positions of authority who are always right no matter what!"[24] In these increasingly corporate healthcare environments, we are continuously ignored and disappointed—left feeling as if we are just left flapping in the wind.

COMPASSION FATIGUE: THE WORST KIND OF BURNOUT

Having worked in large health care organizations in both China and the United States, I have seen so many nurses suffer from a form of burnout called "compassion fatigue"— also known as secondary traumatic stress. This type of stress comes from being overloaded with traumatic and depressing situations beyond our control. Dealing with critical patients, distressed family members, and life-and-death situations is incredibly taxing. Many studies point to the fact that nurses who work in acute care, long-term care, and palliative care settings are particularly prone to burnout.[25, 26, 27, 28]

Over the long haul, it can simply be too much to be the person on the frontlines of life-altering trauma in the ER and ICU, to work with long-term issues such as dementia and mental illness, to provide care for the precious—and precarious—lives in the neonatal ICU, to help those who are suffering from intense pain, and to provide care for both patients and families in hospice settings. I remember clearly how long I was depressed when a twenty-five-year-old cancer patient died right after his surgery, even though we did absolutely everything we could to save him. And I remember clearly the stories of a friend, Donna, who had worked in the neonatal intensive care unit since graduation. After seeing infants pass away or suffer from congenital deformities and traumatic deliveries, she came home and wept. She worried about having her own children, and she saw the families' faces long after they were gone. She was strong for everyone else all day. She had to be. But when even the most prepared, courageous, and stoic nurse witnesses suffering long enough, it definitely takes a toll. One nurse blogger put it this way: "I didn't burnout, I went up in a great big ball of flames."[29]

BRINGING IT HOME

Chronic stress negatively affects your job satisfaction, work performance—and even your life outside of work. A recent study indicated that there is a direct correlation between workplace stress and home-life satisfaction.[30]

With all of the aforementioned difficulties and stressors associated with our profession, it's not surprising that we find our work interfering with our personal life. Nurses can't help but bring their work home with them in many ways: sleep deprivation, disrupted sleep cycles, physical pain, lack of proper nutrition, and—like Donna—not being able to put work behind you after you are done with your shift. In one survey, 82 percent of survey respondents found it difficult to strike a work-life balance, while 28 percent "always" had work on their mind. Only 18 percent were able to "always put family and personal life first."[31] You would think that we nurses might be able to find at least one opportunity in a week to do just one thing we consider fun, but in this survey, an alarming 88 percent of respondents found it "difficult to do something fun at least once a week," while another 30 percent found it "impossible due to being tired and stressed."[32]

So here we are, tired, stressed, and finding it difficult to focus on our personal lives. Even if we aren't thinking about what happened at work, the stress is still lingering in our psyche and body—which affects everyone around us. When you work in an emotionally, mentally, and physically draining environment, your relationships suffer, your children suffer, your entire life suffers.

Most nurses are female, and women have greater home and family obligations. But even those who don't have children aren't off the hook when it comes to burnout! Rates of burnout can actually be higher among single workers and workers with no children if they don't have a strong network of support.[33]

Furthermore, when you work in a depressing, draining, and demanding position—one in which you have no voice, no choice, and no control, while you are continuously responsible for the physical, emotional, and psychological health of others—your entire well-being is at stake. We all know about "nurse's bladder" (the urinary tract and kidney infections that often afflict nurses from a lack of breaks for hydration and elimination), but we are also more prone to illnesses because stress hormones attack our immune system. But it isn't just everyday health issues that we suffer from with our extra stress. Chronic stress can actually cause long-term health problems that aren't so easily cured as a urinary tract infection. One study noted the physiological effects of long-term stress can lead to heart disease, cancer, and chronic pain.[34]

It's no wonder that in a 2011 survey by the American Nurses Association, a whopping 75 percent of the nurses cited the effects of stress and overwork as a top health concern.[35] So many of us are so stressed out from work that it is actually affecting our health for many years to come.

As self-help guru Byron Katie says, "Stress is an alarm clock that lets you know you're attached to something that's not true for you."[36] If you are stressed out, your job is no longer serving you; you are a slave to your job.

IS THIS YOU?

Here are just a few signs that you have had enough stress and are *truly* burned out:

▸ Dreading the thought of going to work. Everyone has days when they would rather be somewhere else, but if you are continually dreading going to work, there may be a problem.

▸ An increase in physical ailments. Burnout can cause an increase in physical problems, such as headaches, stomachaches, and all-over fatigue.

▸ Frequently calling in sick. A sick day now and again is commonplace, but using all your sick time—even when you are not truly sick—can be a sign of burnout.

▸ Boredom. When you are feeling a lack of interest and passion in your work, you start to just "go through the motions." When work isn't challenging or interesting any longer, you are probably burned out.

▸ Becoming easily irritated and frustrated at work. Nurses who suffer from burnout may find they become annoyed more easily with patients, coworkers, and visitors.

▸ Decreased compassion. If you notice you are getting increasingly cynical and are feeling detached from your patients, it could be a sign of burnout.

FINANCIAL WOES

It's not hard to find a job because nurses are so in demand. If you can stick it out, you can retire well. But as we have seen, oftentimes stress isn't worth the pay and nurses quit before they can reap the rewards of their training and degree; sometimes they even quit before they pay back their student loans. With student loan debt for nurses at an all-time high,[37] that's a dangerous proposition.

We are on the very front lines of patient care, but our pay doesn't reflect that. Of course, we don't have the training and education of physicians, but we perform so much more of the hands-on care and carry so many responsibilities. We provide so much physical, medical, mental, and psychosocial support to patients and families. We are effectively social workers, mentors, friends, and problem solvers. I remember one time I had a patient's adult son ranting in the lobby that he was "going to sue that doctor over what he did to my mom!" I was able to defuse the situation by actively and empathetically listening, communicating with him patiently, and communicating with the physician effectively. This type of conflict and chaos is a daily occurrence for nurses. (And, of course, the physician had no idea how I saved his day!) We have no control over the administration's rules, physicians' orders, or other factors, but we are the ones putting out the fires. If only we were truly paid for all we do! I'm not alone here in thinking this: a study from 2014 notes that 40 percent of RNs believe they are not fairly compensated and another 44 percent feel that although they are fairly compensated, they could use additional remuneration. *If you are in the 88 percent who feel that your talents are not being rewarded, I hope you will follow me on the path to success!*[38]

WHAT IF YOU COULD HAVE THE LIFE
YOU ALWAYS DREAMED OF?

So, here you are with no freedom, no respect, and no prosperity. But what if you could use your compassion for others, critical thinking skills, education, communication skills, and energy to transform your life?

I want to assure you: you are not trapped as a nurse—you have all the skills required to become a successful entrepreneur. You really do! If I can do it, so can you.

Imagine what your life would be like:

Feeling respected because your daily work reflects who you truly want to be;

Feeling inner peace because there is time and space to take care of yourself and to be the best you can be;

Feeling powerful because you are completely in charge of your life and achieve your optimal quality of life by serving others;

Feeling hopeful because you can offer so much more to your community;

Feeling proud of yourself because you contribute to your or your family's prosperity;

Feeling loved because you are able to spend quality time with loved ones;

Feeling free because you don't have to ask for someone else's permission;

Feeling confident because you are moving ahead to reach the life goals of your heart's desire;

Feeling lucky because you can catch so many opportunities emerging from today's health care delivery system;

Feeling excited to get up each day to help change so many people's lives optimally.

You can soar beyond your current confusion and struggles. There are so many opportunities!

Chapter Two

So You Want to Be—or Already Are—a Nurse Entrepreneur?

The best time to plant a tree was 20 years ago. The second best time is now.

—Chinese proverb

I CAN SHOW YOU THE WAY! In this book, I will show you how I successfully used my nursing skills to develop my businesses by

1. Cultivating an entrepreneurial mind-set
2. Defining a compassionate purpose
3. Adopting successful habits
4. Being open to receiving all of the abundance of the universe
5. Never giving up

Chapter 5, "What to Play," includes nearly 200 self-employment ideas and information on the most promising opportunities along with profiles of several nurses who found awesome success as entrepreneurs! If you are planning to become an independent case manager, legal nurse consultant or life care planner, which are my specialties, you will find my insights there as well. The remaining chapters outline my four easy steps of success. Most importantly, you will come to understand the surprising ancient Chinese success secret that has informed my entire life and has led me to a peaceful, prosperous, happy life—a secret that stems from true stories about my ancestors' lives, childhood myths that enriched my imagination, ancient proverbs, and more. These are thousands of years of ancient Chinese business wisdom distilled into actionable easy-to-use intelligence for nurse entrepreneurs seeking income, respect, and independence. I find it so interesting that this old stuff from my ancestors in the Far East—their stories, aphorisms, and beliefs—is currently being supported by academia! I have included wisdom and research from current scholars and entrepreneurs as well.

How do you achieve the life you always dreamed of? How do you get what you want most out of your life? The answers are found in the principles of the four easy and solid steps of success described in Part 3.

As you read through this secret, something amazing will begin to connect in you! You will begin to awaken to the potential within you and to unlock your hidden power.

ARE YOU READY FOR THE WONDERFUL CONNECTION?

If you are thinking about self-employment, entrepreneurship, or breaking free of the confines of your nursing career—like I did—you will be pleased to know that there is a growing field with plenty of opportunities for you to use all of the skills and knowledge you possess to create your own destiny.

In most large health care organizations, nurses comprise the largest proportion of the workforce (about 80 percent)[1] and are considered to be integral and indispensable in the health continuum, but we are not considered equal partners in corporate health care systems. It doesn't matter if you are a generalist or a specialist, a rookie or a veteran, just out of college or highly credentialed, our skills and knowledge are underutilized! Our training and talent can be put to better use on our own. But what's out there for us? The International Council of Nurses defines the growing career of "nurse entrepreneur" as a "proprietor of a business that offers nursing services of a direct care, educational, research, administrative or consultative nature."[2] I believe this is absolutely the future of nursing: highly successful nurse staffing company owners, case managers, legal nurse consulting or life care planning business owners, home care business owners, nurse practitioners business owners, independent nurse specialists, case managers, legal nurse consultants, life care planners, visiting nurses and educators, etc. And I also see nurses using their unique gifts and following their true passions by becoming independent entertainers, inventors, and patient coaches. The sky's the limit!

The Bureau of Labor Statistics reports that there are 2.7 million active nursing positions in the United States[3]—and nearly all of these nurses could branch out on their own! Right now, the worldwide health care system is under great pressure because of an aging population, chronic diseases, and high costs.[4] Furthermore there is a lot of confusion and chaos because of changing health care and environmental regulations— and a burgeoning pharmaceutical and durable medical equipment market. A report from the Institute of Medicine's Robert Wood Johnson Foundation Initiative titled *The Future of Nursing: Leading Change, Advancing Health* noted that we nurses have an important contribution to make in building a health care system that will meet the demand for safe, quality, patient-centered, accessible, and affordable care.[5] Given the fact that more and more states have passed laws that allow nurse practitioners to have independent prescriptive authority and full practice authority, this is the best time ever for nurse practitioners to develop a better patient service market to improve access to care for millions.

We can be leaders in a myriad of ways: providing direct care to families, mapping patients' long-term care, educating at-risk populations about healthy lifestyles, advocating and coordinating services for patients, conducting research that will benefit many, inventing products that could save lives, employing other nurses and treating them fairly, or even creating apps that could save on health care costs. There are so many ways that you can fulfill your destiny and care for others.

BUT WAIT, LILY, I AM DOING THIS!

By three methods we may learn wisdom: first, by reflection,
which is noblest; second, by imitation, which is easiest; and third,
by experience, which is the bitterest. —Confucius

Oh boy, I know what you self-employed nurses are feeling right now! You are both excited by hanging out your shingle and in constant doubt: Am I doing enough? Am I growing fast enough? Is there too much competition? Am I good enough? I went through so much of that myself! I have experienced all of the self-doubt and challenges you have, such as:

- ▸ Hiring, training, and supervising employees
- ▸ Managing time effectively
- ▸ Defining products and services
- ▸ Creating marketing plans
- ▸ Managing cash flow
- ▸ Making decisions about capital, reinvesting, and growth expectations
- ▸ Delegating tasks
- ▸ Working effectively with regulators, the health care system, and legal entities
- ▸ Organizing work flow
- ▸ Communicating clearly
- ▸ Navigating lack of growth or even rapid growth

When new challenges arose, I would work too hard, get too little sleep, and ultimately find little joy in life. But whenever I'd get into those "pain patches" of self-doubt, worry, exhaustion, and hyperfocus, I would remind myself of the ancient truths I know about life. Then things would turn around—amazing things would happen at just the right time and prosperity and ease would flow back into my life.

I help my clients realize their goals and work through challenges by helping them with practical nuts and bolts, as well as with the surprising ancient Chinese success secret that I am imparting to you in this book. In the following chapters you will learn about *wu* as well as other ancient Chinese concepts that aid me in maintaining optimism, relaxing mentally and physically, keeping things in proper perspective, having fun, staying open to receiving abundance, being self-reflective and self-aware, and—most importantly—following my instincts, which have never steered me wrong.

Now it's time to see where you are. Is your vision clear and confident—or are you a frog stuck in a well?

Chapter Three

The Deepest Secret Revealed Through a Frog and a Monkey King

....

Looking at the sky from the bottom of the well,
you have a very narrow view.

—Chinese proverb

....

RIGHT NOW, YOU KNOW YOU want to change your life. You think that maybe you can become an entrepreneur somehow. You could, for instance, start your nurse staffing company or home care agency, become an independent case manager or legal nurse consultant, invent a new product, or create your specialty service—and thus be able to reclaim your life, your time, your peace of mind. But you're looking at this prospect wondering: Can I really do this? What if I fail? You tell yourself you are not capable: Entrepreneurship is for other people, not me. I'm not smart enough. I need a million dollars (or another degree) to launch a business. I am too old (or young) to start a business. I'll do it when X finally happens. Remaining miserable is easier than confronting the unknown. You, my friend, are at the bottom of the well.

Imagine there is a well dug into the earth, and there is a frog at the bottom. When the frog looks up, all he sees is the tiny slice of sky afforded by his position in the narrow well. That's all he knows of reality. He doesn't think he can get out, and even if he does, the world is so small—his prospects are so dim. He is frustrated and confused: the well is so deep, how could he ever escape? The world is so small, it may not even be worth the struggle. Imagine if he relied on what he has: his ability to jump. He's always had this, but never thought of using his strengths in a different way. He could finally hop out of the well and onto the earth and look up and look around. He would see that sky is huge, everywhere, and infinite.

This is what you need to know: the world is abundant and infinite. There is never a limit to what you can earn, learn, and achieve. Here is what you also need to know: you possess everything you need to get yourself out of the well. You have a big jangling key ring, and you have all the keys you need to unlock your potential!

Nurses possess amazing critical thinking skills, energy, and drive. We deal with highly critical situations and with highly critical people. We have to prioritize our tasks, keep our emotions in check, think quickly, communicate effectively, solve serious problems, read the energy of a room well, be detail oriented, and work efficiently. All these raw skills are the assets we need to create our businesses. You better believe that every skill I ever acquired as a nurse came in handy when I was building my businesses. When I hired staff, created management systems, researched opportunities, created marketing plans, and communicated with clients, I relied on my strengths honed over the years of working with competing interests, sensitive situations, and at times, chaotic environments. Every skill is a transferrable skill, and believe me, being a nurse prepared me very well for the business world.

We nurses need to wake up to what we can offer. It's in you. In your daily work you juggle so much, smooth so many things out, manage your time and efforts—those are all entrepreneurial skill sets.

But you may be looking at your future prospects like that frog in the well. One tiny disk of light is coming down, and you think that you can't get out of the well. We have to let go of the illusion that we are stuck. Set up a workable goal, a workable plan, a workable environment in order to see how big the sky truly is. It is just so very big. In Chinese they say, *kaikuo yanjie*, broaden your horizons. You know a frog can jump out of the well. But will he?

IS THE CERTAINTY OF MISERY MORE COMFORTING THAN THE MISERY OF UNCERTAINTY?

The greatest question is not whether you have failed, but whether you are content with failure.—Chinese proverb

Oftentimes we see people who are in a miserable situation but choose to stay in it: an unhealthy lifestyle, a toxic job, or a hazardous work environment. Why is this? It is because, for some, the certainty of this misery is more comforting than the misery of uncertainty. The frog knows exactly what to expect in that well; he doesn't have to worry about all of the things that could happen should he jump out.

The greatest attribute for any entrepreneur is to be able to rest comfortably in uncomfortable situations and decisions—whatever they may be. Life is full of awkward, risky, complicated, ambiguous, unusual situations that fill us with fear. We need to hold that fear in the palm of our hands, regard it with curiosity and respect, then forge ahead anyway. It is a good thing to have fear! The best outcomes come from the person who has the most fear. I don't know if you have noticed this, but I've noticed that some newly graduated doctors have an attitude of "I know everything," and these are the ones who often make the biggest mistakes. I remember warning one cocky new surgeon performing an appendectomy, "Look, be careful. I have seen what can go wrong." The veteran doctors, on the other hand, know that it is wise to be cautious and fearful because they've seen that anything can go wrong—no matter how they prepare themselves and even if they do their absolute best. Confidence is one thing, but embracing the fear that anything could go wrong is important for an optimal outcome.

Becoming an entrepreneur doesn't need to be an uncertainty if you do the best preparation. In *The Art of War*, a Chinese military treatise written by Sun Tzu in the fifth century BC, it says that if you want to win the battle, you have to be close to your enemies. You have to understand them, let yourself feel a little calm in the middle of that. It's okay to have no solution in the middle of the fear. Get to know your enemy, and then you can create your battle strategies. It's not about avoiding fear or having no fear but embracing fear and being prepared to take the challenge, confront the fear, and defeat the fear.

EMBRACE THE CAREGIVER IN YOU

You, yourself, as much as anybody in the entire universe,
deserve your love and affection.—Buddha

As a nurse you are already in the nurse's caregiver mode: with great strength and resolve, you attend to the needs of your patients, families, partners, parents, community—and even the doctors and administrators. As you embark on this journey of entrepreneurship, I want you to embrace the caregiver in you by adding one more person to this list: you. By being your own boss, you will be able to take control over your own time, resources, and mental space for self-care. This may sound selfish, but it is not. You are here on this earth to become the most self-actualized version of yourself that you can be—and when you tenderly and consistently care for your dreams, your body, and your mind, you are able to shine brightly and live in peace and prosperity.

A PURPOSE-DRIVEN ENTREPRENEURSHIP

Every step leaves a footprint.—Chinese proverb

Here's the thing: self-care prepares us for the purpose of caring for others! We nurses aren't hardwired simply for our own success; we have a higher calling. In a 2014 study of the job satisfaction of RNs, almost all of the nurses reported that the main factor that influenced their job satisfaction was being involved with patient care and focusing on patients' problems. One nurse said, "When I help my patients with their needs and problems, I feel happy, and this makes me feel satisfied."[1] What satisfies us most is having a higher calling!

I have so much that propelled me to work hard: my clients, my family, and my ancestors. I try to carry on my grandparents' legacy of creativity, entrepreneurship, and wisdom. There was something so much bigger than me to hold onto and push me. At the end of the day, it wasn't about money or power or fancy things. It was about my child's future and my ancestors' past. It was about providing quality services for individuals and families and making an optimal impact by serving others. It was about building a better world.

Leadership and business expert Ronald Heifetz said, "If you find what you do each day seems to have no link to any higher purpose, you probably want to rethink what you're doing."[2] It is usually easier for those who provide direct care, like teachers, nurses, first responders, and social workers, to see the immediate fruits of their labors—and to feel the purpose of their daily work. You may wonder if you could feel a strong enough sense of purpose as a business owner who works in an office with long-term goals. I think about a friend who is a very conscientious and driven small-business owner of an accounting firm; crunching all of those numbers may not seem like a higher calling, but she explained that when she does her job well, the business, her clients, and her employees succeed. In the big picture she is contributing to the livelihood of countless families—and to the economy of the entire community. That is what she holds onto when she is doing tedious daily work.

IT CAN'T BE JUST ABOUT MONEY

A satisfied person is happy even if he/she is poor; a dissatisfied person is sad even if he/she is rich.—*Chinese proverb*

Some people think that their purpose could be big homes, vacations, and luxury cars. And certainly, riches will come! But to hold onto wealth as a purpose—as your guiding force—is self-defeating.

In fact, decades of research indicates that external rewards such as money, praise, awards, fame, and perks will motivate people to an extent—but there are some drawbacks. In his groundbreaking tome, *Drive: The Truth about What Motivates Us and Why*, researcher Daniel Pink claims that being rewarded merely with wealth can "extinguish intrinsic (internal) motivation," "diminish performance," "crush creativity," and "foster short-term thinking."[3] Pink notes that what we are truly, sustainably motivated by autonomy, mastery, and purpose.[4]

If we are merely grasping for the gold, we have lost the true purpose of life. Life's riches come in creativity, expression, relationships, and service—in other words: the work we do. Humorist Leo Rosten said it best: "The purpose of life is not to be happy—but . . . to be productive, to be useful, to have it make some difference that you lived at all."[5] And when you are productive and useful, you will achieve peace—which will ultimately bring you both wealth and joy to achieve your optimal quality of life.

So, while you are working on your new business, what will you hold onto? Who will benefit in the long run from your efforts? When you are creating marketing strategies, attracting new clients, or making lead calls, it may not feel immediately rewarding. But when you have created a successful, flourishing business that employs many and rewards you, and in turn your family, with more time, freedom, dignity, prosperity, and peace, it will definitely feel rewarding. What will you work for? Is it time with loved ones? Is it making your community healthier? Is it being able to care for your own mental and physical health? Embrace the caregiver within you to become a successful nurse entrepreneur of this distinctive new era!

MONKEY KING MIND

The tree will need to face more wind on its way to getting bigger, and it will have to face the most wind when it's the biggest!—Chinese proverb

You may hear that the entrepreneur is the loneliest person in the world. I certainly think that people may fear by being very different and rebellious against the fixed "normal" ways of thinking.

There definitely is a certain mind-set that successful entrepreneurs possess that distinguishes them from others. Literally thousands of books have been written about this unique entrepreneurial mind-set, and I have read quite a few of them. They usually say the same thing about what it takes to be successful:

- **Be fearless.** Notice your fear, embrace it, and charge ahead anyway. See challenges—and even challenging people—as opportunities.

- **See the world as abundant.** Competition, for instance, should be seen as data—not a threat—because there is enough wealth to go around.

- **Be creative.** Think outside the box, do things differently, don't stick with the status quo.

- **Take risks.** With great risk comes great reward. If you fail or make a mistake, learn from it!

- **Be curious.** Research, wonder, and ask questions. Success comes from knowledge gained by an insatiable curiosity, not necessarily a formal education.

- **Be detail-oriented.** Big things are made from small components that have been carefully built, not from grand schemes that don't include the minute details.

- **Don't sweat the small stuff.** Perfection is the enemy of progress.

- **Work hard.** There are no shortcuts to success, but with great effort you will inevitably see the fruits of your labor.

- **Know your limitations.** Seek out mentors and specialists and don't be afraid to ask questions and get outside perspectives!

- **Follow your passion.** Do what you love and figure out a way to get paid for it. Everyone is called to do something!

- **Be an entrepreneur all the time.** You don't do entrepreneurship as a job; it is your identity and a way of life.

- **Be decisive.** Taking risks, making hard decisions, and working with difficult people are all part of the process, so you may as well get accustomed to being strong in sticky situations.

I'll expand on many of those points later. I believe that each and every one of our nurses can become wildly successful at what we do if we possess a successful mind-set.

There is a Chinese idiom that goes like this: *Su da zhao feng*, or "The tree will need to face more wind on its way to getting bigger." And it will have to face the most wind when it's the biggest! Perhaps this is the cause of loneliness: you are standing there all alone bracing against the gusts. Indeed, I've faced those winds. I certainly remember when, in my twenties, I founded and built the Cosmetic Surgery and Women's Health business in Guilin, China, just as the city had opened its doors to the world. Even with my track record of proven success, the struggles were very real when I tried to convince the city authorities that privately owned organizations would be higher quality and an asset to the future of the health care market. I was literally going up against the forces of the established authority, and yet I didn't want to settle for less. I was determined to set up my own marketing and operating systems to provide optimal service to my patients and clients.

What was it that kept me persevering through all of the adversities and challenges along the way? Through all the years of my life, I found quite a bit of truth in the classical Chinese stories which lead me define real entrepreneurship. And when I think of the true qualities of an entrepreneur, I think of the famous ancient Chinese stories of the Monkey King, *Xi You ji*, that my grandparents loved to read. As you read this summary of the legend, please think carefully about not only the moral of the story but the qualities that the Monkey King possesses. This story has served me well.

THE GENIUS OF MONKEY KING

I'm small, but I can GROW easily enough
—Sun Wukong, Monkey King

Monkey King, *Sun Wukong*, is one of the most widely known Chinese characters in the famous novel *Journey to the West*, or *Hsi Yu Chi*. Written during the Ming Dynasty (c. 1500–1582), the story is based on the real-life journeys of the monk Xuan Zang, who traveled on foot to India to seek the Buddhist holy books, the sutras. After accomplishing his goal, he walked back to China, translated the sutras into Chinese, and made a significant contribution to the development of Buddhism in China. His tales are a combination of folklore, religion, allegory, history, and satire. But it is not the monk's profound story that is so engaging to the audience; it is the intrepid and courageous Monkey King that captures our hearts. He is rebellious, indefatigable, ingenious, indestructible, righteous, and humorous.

THE LEGEND OF MONKEY KING

According to this legend, Monkey King was born out of a rock fertilized by the grace of Heaven and Earth. He was taught magic (gongfu) by an immortal Taoist master. The brilliant monkey could transform himself into seventy-two different images of such things as a tree, a bird, a beast of prey, or an insect that can sneak into an enemy's body to fight him from the inside. Also each of his hairs held magical properties, making each capable of being transformed into clones of the Monkey King himself, or into various weapons, animals, and other objects. He also knew spells that could command wind and water and could conjure protective circles against demons, or even command demons themselves. When needed, he could travel 108,000 miles with a single somersault—using clouds as a vehicle. He was also very strong, lifting up to nine tons.

Monkey King proclaimed himself to be the only king, defying the Great Emperor of Jade (Yù Huáng Dà Dì)—who was the recognized authority over the heaven, the seas, the earth, and the underworld. That act of treason, along with the protests of the masters of the four seas and Hell, sent forth a relentless assault of the Heavenly Army. But Monkey King fought his way into the ocean, defeated the Dragon King, and captured a large, gold-banded iron rod, which he used to ballast the waves. This became Monkey King's most prized possession and favorite weapon because the rod could expand or shrink at his command. He used it ingeniously in many encounters. Once, for instance, Monkey King stormed into Hell and defeated the Hadean King with the rod and was granted eternal life for himself and all of his followers.

Throughout the legend, there are many confrontations with the Heavenly Army, but Monkey King always came out on top. After suffering too many crushing and humiliating defeats, the celestial monarch decided to offer the monkey an official title in Heaven—but with little real authority. After learning that he was just a figurehead and an object of ridicule with no actual power, Monkey King revolted and fought his way back to Earth to reclaim his original self-proclaimed title of King. The Heavenly Army eventually enlisted the help of all the warrior gods, and with a variety of tricks, they managed to capture the elusive monkey. Monkey was sentenced to death but no method of murder worked on him! With his bronze head and iron shoulders, the monkey repelled strikes and dulled swords. Finally, the emperor commands that he be thrown into the fiery furnace where the Taoist minister Tai Shang Lao Jun created his pills of immortality. But instead of killing Monkey King, the fire and smoke only served to sharpen his eyes so that he could see through things that others cannot. Yet again, he fought his way back to Earth—this time even stronger.

After he could stand no more humiliation at the hands of this seemingly immortal being, the celestial emperor implored Buddha for his assistance. Buddha placed the monkey under a great mountain known as Wu Zhi Shan (The Mount of the enormous weight of Five Fingers) and leaves him there—thinking it the perfect prison. But the monkey survived. After five hundred years, the monk Xuan Zang came to his rescue.

Fortunately, Buddha had arranged for Monkey King to become the monk's escort to the West in order to retrieve the Sutras. On their way to India, two more disciples, also at the will of the Buddha, joined the group: a silly and courageous pig—who had been transformed from a celestial general because had drunkenly assaulted a fairy, and a sea monster who also was transformed from an exiled celestial general. Both were atoning for prior transgressions. They were later joined by a horse—himself an incarnation of a dragon prince. The five of them begin their tumultuous journey to India—a journey packed with adventures and trials that demonstrate the prowess of the monk's four disciples, especially Monkey King. The group encountered a series of eighty-one tribulations before accomplishing their mission and returning safely to China. There, Monkey King, Sun Wukong, was granted Buddhahood for his service and strength.

Monkey King has the superpower of a spirit, and is able to do unbelievable magic; meanwhile, he has the emotions of a human, knowing precisely whom or what to love or hate. He also possesses the piety of a disciple. He bore a lot of pains on the road to seek the Sutra without shaking his loyalty. It is the combination of righteousness, braveness, faithfulness, and humor that makes Monkey King a beloved household character and the symbol of the righteous power to fight all monsters and evil forces.

I had to adopt a Monkey King mind in order to accomplish my entrepreneurial goals, and believe me, it wasn't easy or natural for me. You see, Monkey King is rebellious, resilient, resourceful, clever, and full of joy, and he thinks big—so big that he proclaims he is king! But I grew up in a typical Chinese city during and after the cultural revolution, when everyone was strict and quite restrained, and my teachers implored me to be subordinate, to fit in, and to not make waves. (Let's be honest, doctors and administrators can be quite demanding as well!) However, in order to create a successful cosmetic surgery and women's health business, I had to stand up to the local authority, create a plan on a grand scale, convince others to believe in me, get back up when I was knocked down, and do it all with a smile on my face because of a deep sense of purpose and joy. I had to completely change my closed, fixed mind-set—my "I don't want to make others upset" mind-set—and be utterly indefatigable, brave, righteous, and full of determination to succeed. I had to have a Monkey King mind-set. This new way of thinking may come even easier for you here in this free and brave country. For me, this Monkey King mind-set came, and it has become more and more normal and natural.

MODERN SCIENCE PROVES MONKEY KING RIGHT

When I let go of what I am, I become what I might be.—Lao Tzu

After decades of research on achievement and success, world-renowned Stanford University psychologist Carol Dweck discovered what Monkey King already knew: it is not just our abilities and talent that bring us success, but whether we approach our goals with a fixed or growth mind-set. In a fixed mind-set, people believe their basic qualities, like talent, personality, or intelligence, are just fixed traits that they were born with. They spend their time documenting, demonstrating, or proving their existing traits rather than developing them any further. They believe that the brain doesn't change or improve after a certain time frame. They also believe that talent alone will create success, without real effort. They're wrong.

In a growth mind-set, people believe that their most basic abilities can be developed through dedication and hard work—brains and talent are just the starting point. This attitude of growth fosters a sense of curiosity, resilience, and positive outlook on challenges and setbacks that is absolutely essential for success. Most great people have this growth mind-set and thus the traits of grit, love of learning, and ability to learn from—and even enjoy—a challenge.[6]

In her seminal research, Dr. Dweck had 400 fifth-graders attempt to solve puzzles. With one set of children, the research assistant would praise the child on her supposed innate ability to solve the problem stating a single line: "You must be smart at this."[7] And with the other set of children the researcher would praise the child's effort with a single line: "You must have worked really hard."[8]

The students were then given a choice of tests for the second round. One choice was a puzzle that would be more difficult than the first, and the researchers told the kids that they'd be more difficult but that they'd learn a lot from attempting the puzzles. The other choice was an easy test, nearly identical to the first. Of those children who were praised for their effort, 90 percent chose the harder set of puzzles! The majority of children of who were praised for their intelligence chose the easy test. The so-called smart kids took the cop out! Why? Dweck explains: "When we praise children for their intelligence . . . we tell them that this is the name of the game: Look smart, don't risk making mistakes."[9] And that's what the fifth graders did: they chose to look smart and avoid the risk of embarrassment. They were cultivating a fixed mind-set.

THE FEARLESSNESS, PLAYFULNESS, AND TENACITY OF THE MONKEY KING

"Here I am, only four hundred years old," said the Monkey King, "and I've already reached the heights of greatness. What is left to hope and strive for? What can be higher than a king?"

"Your Majesty," said the gibbon carefully, "we have ever been grateful for that time four centuries ago when you hatched from the stone, wandered into our midst, and found for us this hidden cave behind the waterfall. We made you our king as the greatest honor we could bestow. Still, I must tell you that kings are not the highest of beings."

"They're not?" said the Monkey King.

"No, Your Majesty." Above them are gods, who dwell in Heaven and govern Earth. Then there are Immortals, who have gained great powers and live forever. And finally there are Buddhas and Bodhisattva, who have conquered illusion and escaped rebirth."

"Wonderful!" cried the Monkey King. "Maybe I can become all three!" He considered a moment, then said, "I think I'll start with the Immortals. I'll search all the earth until I've found one, then learn to become one myself!"

—Excerpt from *Monkey King: A Superhero Tale of China* Aaron Shepard[20]

In a subsequent round, none of the fifth graders had a choice. The test was difficult, designed for kids two years ahead of their grade level. Predictably, everyone failed. But again, the two groups of children, divided at random at the study's start, responded differently. Those praised for their effort on the first test assumed they simply hadn't focused hard enough on this test. Dweck recalls: "They got very involved, willing to try every solution to the puzzles. . . . Many of them remarked, unprovoked, 'This is my favorite test.'"[10] But those who were praised for their smarts? They assumed their failure was proof that they weren't really smart after all. "Just watching them, you could see the strain. They were sweating and miserable."[11]

Having artificially induced a round of failure, Dweck's researchers then gave all of the children a final round of puzzles that were purposely created to be as easy as the first round of puzzles. The children who had been initially praised for their effort significantly improved on their first score—by about 30 percent! Those who'd been praised for their intelligence did worse than they had at the very beginning—by about 20 percent![12] Their scores went way down. What they believed about themselves impacted their performance significantly! You see, when they thought that they had no control over their ability to learn, and that it was fixed and unchangeable, they not only wouldn't take risks, they would fail when they tried. But when they believed that they had control over their destiny—over what their brains could accomplish—they thrived!

Similar research has been conducted on adults in corporations, schools, and small businesses yielding similar results.[13] Those individuals and organizations who firmly believe that "people are just born with 'it,'" fail miserably, while those people and organizations who believe that certain powerful traits such as leadership, problem-solving, and communication skills can be fostered and developed—even in the face of major conflicts and challenges—tended to grow.[14]

What does this all mean for you as an entrepreneur? It means that we received messages in school, at home, at work, in society, and told ourselves that only certain people have the goods to get ahead—that if you weren't born into a certain genetic pool you were destined to be what you believe yourself to be. This is wrong on so many levels.

First of all, you can cultivate anything—your talents, outlook, personality, habits, and your intellect—whatever! Your brain and body are malleable and improvable. It doesn't matter whether you have fancy degrees or are very young or very old. In fact, researchers now know that the brain continues to develop new neural pathways until an advanced age! We have new understandings every day; Every day we are smarter and wiser. It's amazing how much we grow!

Secondly, many of us were praised by our well-meaning teachers, parents, and coaches as being smart, star athletes, talented, and the like. This actually set us up to be afraid of failing. If we failed, then we might not have that perceived attribute any longer; we would be seen as failures instead. We would be letting everyone down and losing that status. But failing is the hallmark of trying! I think of something that Sara Blakely, founder of Spanx and the world's youngest self-made female billionaire, said about her childhood: "My dad encouraged us to fail. Growing up, he would ask us what we failed at that week. If we didn't have something, he would be disappointed. It changed my mindset at an early age that failure is not the outcome. Don't be afraid to fail."[15] Her dad didn't praise her as being smart; his measure of success was what she had attempted. Embrace the process of trying!

Thirdly, you can embrace the attitude that challenges are simply opportunities for growth and learning. Personally, when I have yet another challenge come my way, I am like that little boy who said, "This is my favorite test!" Every time I meet an obstacle, I relish the chance to learn something new, sharpen some skill, develop my grit, and grow more deeply into who I can become. It is essentially about humility (which I will touch on later in the book). When you know that you do not know all of the answers, you feel as if you have nothing to lose and everything to gain. I hope you, too, will take on every challenge with a curious smile and the attitude of "This is my favorite test!"

CULTIVATING THE MONKEY KING MIND-SET

- **Enjoy the process.** Monkey King is interested in the moment at hand; whether he achieves the goal has nothing to do with his self-worth or his enjoyment of the process. That doesn't mean you don't care if you reach your goal—of course you care. But in the big picture, it doesn't matter what the outcome is so long as you enjoyed the process and gave it your all.

- **Use your imagination.** When you address a problem or begin a task, take a moment to envision your brain literally changing—because that is truly what happens when you think! Just as Monkey King can shrink and grow, so can you.

- **Cultivate a sense of purpose.** When Monkey King, the monk, and the rest of the team go west for the sutras, Monkey King wisely uses his skills. Earlier in the story he doesn't have a purpose; he is merely having fun and learning new skills, not really accomplishing anything of merit. Keep in the back of your mind the real reason you are working toward a goal.

- **Try different learning tactics.** According to the legend, when Monkey King learns *gong fu* he goes about it in an entirely new way and quickly surpasses his master. There's no one-size-fits-all model for learning. What works for one person may not work for you.

- **Use the word "yet."** "Yet" is one of my favorite words! "I don't know how to do that yet." "I haven't mastered this new technology yet." When I use "yet," I know that I haven't mastered it, attained it, understood it, but I certainly will. Monkey King knows it will eventually happen, and so do I.

- **Stand proud and tall, literally.** Harvard researcher Amy Cuddy found that standing in a confident pose for two minutes before attempting something new or challenging improves the outcome significantly.[16] So before you meet with your first client, give your first sales speech, stand like a superhero, or like a CEO, and notice the difference. If you need a model of what this looks like, just look at the drawing of Monkey King—now, that's confidence!

- **View challenges as opportunities.** When there is a new, sticky, or troubling situation—or even a troubling person, Monkey King never backs down. I am so very grateful for every challenge thrown my way because it is another opportunity for me to become stronger and wiser. Randy Pausch in *The Last Lecture* sees it this way: "The brick walls are there for a reason. The brick walls are not there to keep us out. The brick walls are there to give us a chance to show how badly we want something. Because the brick walls are there to stop the people who don't want it badly enough. They're there to stop the other people."[17]

- **View criticism as feedback, not the end of the world.** When someone criticizes your ideas or work, it is a cause for gratitude. It is new information on how to improve your game.

- **Be patient with yourself.** We are our worst taskmasters and critics. Don't throw in the towel if you don't get the results you want quickly enough. Sure, Monkey King sometimes is an impatient, silly monkey, but in the big picture, he is very patient. The journey to the west took fourteen years and many trials along the way—but he never gave up.

- **Be humble.** It is only when Monkey King has learned humility that he is given true freedom. Be soft and humble with your interactions with others, as no one is perfect or perfectly wise. I find that the most humble people I know have accomplished the most but refuse to toot their own horn.

- **Emphasize growth over speed.** Don't ask how long something took you; ask how much you have learned or grew in the process! Sure, while Monkey King can do a somersault of 108,000 miles, the most meaningful journey—and his true life's mission—took fourteen years. Faithful and steady truly wins the race.

- **Replace the word "failing" with the word "learning."** If you start a business and it isn't successful right away, you aren't failing—you are learning how not to run a business so that you can learn how to run it well in the future! When Thomas Edison was asked about all of his failed attempts at creating a light bulb, he famously replied, "I have not failed. I've just found 10,000 ways that won't work." When Monkey King was trapped under the Five Finger Mountain for 500 years, he didn't fail; he learned how to be patient, humble, and of service to others.

- **Like Monkey King, take risks in the company of others.** When you don't take yourself too seriously, and openly take risks—when you even risk failing—in front of others, it will become easier and easier to take more risks in the future.

- **Reflect on your growth.** This is a *huge* mistake people make when they are on a journey. Whether starting a business, designing a new marketing plan, or working on a project, don't forget to take time to reflect on how far you have come and how much you have changed. If you are pressed for time, just make a scratch list. You can also just try to envision a scene in your mind of how you used to be. By noticing the changes and improvements you are less likely to be discouraged. Monkey King's group came back with the sutras—all of the Buddha's wisdom. He also came back with a story that illustrated how much he had changed.

- **Celebrate your actions, not your awards.** If you truly appreciate growth, you'll want to share your progress with others. Celebrating external rewards or showy milestones can actually discourage you unless—as part of that celebration—you discuss and reflect on the efforts that got you to that point. When Monkey King is granted Buddhahood, he bows because it is a celebration of his awareness and growth.

- **Stop seeking approval.** Just like Monkey King, who doesn't care even what the celestial monarch thinks, you will only be successful if you care about what you think by your own measures. Virginia Woolf said: "The eyes of others our prisons; their thoughts our cages."[18] Do not be in the prison of others' thoughts.

- **It all comes down to being absolutely fearless.** Monkey King is afraid of nobody and nothing. *Webster's* defines "fear" as "an unpleasant emotion caused by the belief that someone or something is dangerous, likely to cause pain, or a threat." Analyze your fears by writing them down and asking if there is a real danger if you attempt to climb this wall or start this journey. You will realize that it is not the danger that is holding you back but your false beliefs about the danger. Then ask yourself: are you actually afraid to become magnificent? Writer Marianne Williamson says: "Our deepest fear is not that we are inadequate. Our deepest fear is that we are powerful beyond measure. It is our light, not our darkness, that most frightens us."[19] Embrace your fear! Let your light shine!

Here in America there is also a strong sense of playing it safe, resting on our laurels, fitting in, and not thinking outside the box. But you will come to realize that the little voice inside your head that keeps saying "no!" is actually just your conditioning and your upbringing. You will come to realize some of your friends, family, and naysayers (like the Army of the Heavens) have *their* reality, but you can embrace a completely different mentality. You just need some confidence and some vision. You just need to stop being a stuck frog and start being like a clever Monkey King so that you can start getting into the game.

Part 2:

GET INTO
THE GAME

Chapter Four

More Than
Monkeying Around

....

A journey of a thousand miles begins with just one step.
—Lao Tzu

....

YOU MAY BE ASKING: "HOW exactly do I go from being a discouraged frog stuck in a well to a happy Monkey King who only finds good fortune?" Well, you certainly can't snap your fingers and make it happen magically. You must create a plan. Success is by design. You already have the critical thinking skills from nursing school and your work. You are excellent at assessing, analyzing, prioritizing, reasoning, identifying, communicating, implementing, researching, evaluating, and more. You now need to cultivate what you have with great intention.

To illustrate this, here's a little story: When I was recruited to play for my school's volleyball team in Guilin, my coach, Mr. Zhao, said, "Lily, this will change your life." I didn't believe him, of course; I just thought it was a fun sport to try. And while I didn't have any good experience with the sport (I hadn't even played in gym class!), and I was even a little afraid of sports (having broken my elbow playing soccer as a child), I did possess many of the skills and requirements of a good volleyball player: I was tall, fast, and strong—with good eye-hand coordination. But in order to transform into an excellent player, I had to create a plan for success. I certainly couldn't grow taller, but I could get faster, stronger, more agile, and gain more muscle memory and eye-hand coordination. I wrote down my plans: wake up at five every morning, climb the Elephant Trunk Hill, lift weights at the school gym, and practice every day. I was just a teenager, and you better believe that I didn't want to wake up early and feel all of the pain and exhaustion from the workouts. But as I followed my plan, I noticed changes: I really did begin to improve my game. Eventually I became the setter—the most important position on the team—truly, the soul of the team. From this role, I learned leadership skills, communication skills, perseverance, and confidence. I learned that setting a goal, and following it through, truly pays off. I believe that I still feel the benefits of this transformation emotionally, physically, and mentally. Mr. Zhao was right!

I know, I know: being a setter on a volleyball team is low stakes. It is a very small risk to try out a sport where I could succeed or fail, and it really didn't mean too much in the long run. Starting a business is an entirely different ball game, right? There is real money, real time, and a real personal reputation on the line. But you know, I believe those volleyball skills of goal setting, organization, communication, and leadership are really the same skills that I needed to succeed in my businesses.

Think about your life experience. Have you ever planned a party or trip? Have you ever had to organize a project or complete a course? Have you ever had to lead a workshop or a community club? Have you ever had to persevere over some obstacle or through a difficult time? Of course you have! Those same low-stakes endeavors are just like starting and running a successful business. And when you really think about it, nursing is much more high stake than running a business. Think of all the times you had to quickly evaluate and assess, then make critical decisions about patients. Think of all the times you had to communicate effectively and diplomatically with others. Think of all the times you had to be confident, efficient, and professional.

You have what it takes; all you need is to cultivate your existing leadership and critical thinking skills and fearlessly start your own nursing business. All you need is to get in the game. As basketball player Michael Jordan famously said, "I can accept failure, everyone fails at something. I can't accept not trying."[1] And I know, once you start on this journey, you may, like me, find it to be so infinitely peaceful, joyful, and prosperous that you'll wonder why you ever questioned starting it!

GETTING YOUR BRAIN GAME ON

Can you imagine what I would do if I could do all I can?
—Sun Tzu, The Art of War

So far, I hope you have realized that:

▸ You need a change in your life.
▸ You possess the critical thinking skills and diverse experiences necessary to become independent and build a business.
▸ You can develop your entrepreneurial mind-set.
▸ Now is the best time to get into the game!
▸ As you start your business or build your existing business, it will be fun!

But what game to play? What business to start? Nurse entrepreneurs may create an entirely new service, improve an existing service, or kick-start a new company or independent service. Nurse entrepreneurship involves recognizing opportunities to make a difference to patient care and finding a way to achieve this. It also involves capitalizing on your existing expertise, interests, talents, and skills.

You may have an idea brewing.

You may have thought: "Hey, I love caring for infants, and I know so much about it—and these parents seem so unsure of themselves! I could make home visits to nervous new parents. It would be a win-win! Heck, maybe I could create an entirely new kind of staffing agency, and that would be a win-win-win!"

Or maybe you are a cardiac nurse who loves to cook locally produced, fresh produce—and thought about hosting a healthy cooking and living retreat for elderly cardiac care patients. What a fun, and possibly lucrative, idea!

That is oftentimes how it happens: you combine a couple interests you are passionate about, and voila! You have an amazing new business! That is what happened to me in Guilin, China. I noticed a need for both skin care and surgical cosmetic services in the area, so I thought, "Why not?" After realizing that our demographic was mostly female, when the business income stream was stable, I decided to add women's health care to the practice by bringing in a few OB-GYN specialists. What we created was a niche service unlike any other in our area—one that catered to the unique needs of women. It was wildly successful.

Entrepreneurial visionary Napoleon Hill boldly claimed, "You can be anything you want to be, if only you believe with sufficient conviction and act in accordance with your faith; for whatever the mind can conceive and believe, the mind can achieve."[2] I truly believe this, because everything that I believed could come true has come true. I believed I could start and build my own successful business, and I did. I believed I could move to America on my own and create a new life, and I did. I believed I could run and grow a prosperous life plan elder law practice, and I did. I believed that I would want to do something really nice for nurses, and I am doing that now.

What have you conceived?

Have you had a thought?

▸ People say you are so good at caring for people with congestive heart failure or diabetes, so you have a desire to set up a chronic disease care center, or

▸ You are so passionate about navigating elderly people in today's health care delivery maze and think that your own medical case management company would be a great fit, or

▸ You love legal shows and movies and think that you could do better by having your own legal nurse consulting service to help people in need, or

▸ You love yoga and think that being an RN and yoga studio owner/teacher/trainer would be a great niche, or

▸ You have a really cool idea for a gadget that could save time in the surgical theater, or

▸ Young people really need comprehensive education about their bodies, and you have a neat idea for a visiting program at middle schools, or

▸ You're pretty tech savvy, and you could consult for a medical software firm, or any number of other ideas.

If you have ever had an expansive, outside-the-box thought of creating, building, leading, healing, performing, teaching, fixing, writing, serving, communicating, organizing, or helping in an entirely new way—or even in an existing way—then you can achieve it!

In the next chapter, I have listed hundreds entrepreneurial ideas for nurses, but before you peruse those pages, ask yourself the following questions:

- What do people tell me I'm good at?
- What am I passionate about at work?
- What am I passionate about outside of work?
- What population would I like to serve?
- What would I like my day to look like in terms of hours, environment, travel requirements, and people with whom I work?
- Would I like to work independently or be the leader of an organization?
- Where would I like to work, in my home, or out of home?
- What idea have I had in the past for serving people, improving services, making people's life easier, and making the world a better place?

I want you to look inside yourself to envision what you want your life to look like; whatever the mind can conceive and believe, the mind can achieve. I know that in my particular case, I craved plenty of time to be with my family and my business. But I also wished to spend more time volunteering in the community, at church, and at school. And I knew from past experiences when I may have overdone it that I required time for self-care, which, for me, means walks with neighbors, lunches with friends, cooking healthy meals, going to yoga class, as well as reading, swimming, and meditating.

I talk a little about my daily practice of meditation in the chapter 6, but I'd like to mention here what business magnate Russell Simmons has to say about the benefits of meditating when it comes to envisioning entrepreneurial opportunities. He says that struggling entrepreneurs grapple with "What kind of void can I fill? What service can I provide? You might think that everything has been done, but if you're a true meditator, and if you're a person who has an open, free spirit, you'll see that the world's done nothing. And you can create tons of stuff that they need. . . . There is a vast space of things that are not done."[3] That is reassuring.

Take some time right now to assess your own strengths, interests, and visions for your future, and then take some time to quiet your mind and allow the creative ideas to flow in. Be open and free. Be playful!

If any of the ideas in the next chapter strike your fancy, make a list of them as well. Mull them over. If any idea that comes to you feels invigorating, or if anything that comes to you seems that it would make the world a better place for us all, that may just be your future talking!

Chapter Five

What to Play?

AN OVERVIEW OF OPPORTUNITIES

....

*Choose a job you love, and you will never have to
work a day in your life.*

—Confucius

....

IN THE FOLLOWING PAGES I feature some promising self-employment
or entrepreneurial ideas for you. I also have a long list of other exciting business
opportunities specifically for those with a specialty background—everything
from acupuncturist to yogi. My entrepreneurial specialties happen to be case
management, legal nurse consulting, life care and advance care planning for the
aging population. (Please see chapter 6, "My Expertise," for my insight into those
particular opportunities. Case management and life care planning are particularly
hot careers right now—with our health care system in chaos and aging baby
boomers—this specialty will be needed more than ever![1, 2] After this section, I have
included interesting profiles of some nurses who followed unique career paths. They
succeeded, I succeeded, and believe me, if we can do it, so can you!

One positive aspect is that you can start by dipping your toe in the water—trying
out one or two ideas before you fully commit. Many nurse entrepreneurs begin following
their passions part time and then work their way to full-time self-employment. When

you read the profiles of successful nurse entrepreneurs, you will notice that many started out "moonlighting," but their second job took off and eclipsed their day job!

There are some very outside-the-box career choices for nurses. I have seen nurse comedians who make us all laugh at conventions, nurses who have their own radio shows, and amazing nurse poets. I believe that everyone should follow his or her bliss! Generally speaking, a nurse entrepreneur is the owner of a business or an independent nurse that offers nursing services of a direct care, educational, research, administrative, or consultative nature. These opportunities are ones in which you will be relying on your nursing background the most and are usually more conventional—yet they are still quite exciting and promising because, under our leadership, we will be modernizing the health care system and creating positive changes.[3]

The best part is that the startup cost for most of these opportunities is relatively low. You probably have a computer, smartphone, printer, and space in your home. You already are licensed to practice as a nurse, so take advantage of everything at your disposal to succeed on your own!

It is helpful to understand what it is that both private individuals and businesses need from a qualified nursing professional.

Private individuals:

▶ Patients require a committed health care professional to create an individualized treatment plan that provides and promotes ongoing wellness.

▶ Patients may require in-home care or temporary care—in an institution, at home, at school, or when traveling.

▶ Patients and their families need someone with knowhow to provide them with customized medical and nursing education for a variety of issues, including perinatal and infant care, disabilities, and chronic ailments.

▶ Family members of a patient might want someone who can review the care being provided to a patient and can suggest ways of improving on that care for the patient's long-term safety and well-being.

▶ Patients or their family members might want a qualified medical auditor to review their medical billing to ensure that all of the charges listed were actually as coded.

▶ Healthy patients may want to create a life care plan before they actually need it.

▶ Some families and individuals may want on-call nursing services for a range of situations, maybe either by phone or by phone/tablet app.

▶ Some individuals would benefit from retreats, workshops, classes, or health vacations designed for their particular needs.

Businesses:

▶ Health care facilities may need the consulting services of a seasoned professional who can observe, analyze, and solve any issues or inefficiencies.

▶ Health care facilities may require permanent or temporary health care staffing services, research, or supervision of projects.

▶ Corporations, lawyers, government agencies, and small businesses outside the health care industry might require your expertise in a variety of ways such as reviewing cases, procedures, or products—or reviewing documents, marketing plans, or facilities.

▶ Many times nurses create their own entirely new procedure, product, or policy. You could bring your new innovations directly to institutions or bring them to market (see chapter 6 for how to get your idea to market).

▶ Many nurses have created independent laboratories, staffing agencies, case management or legal nurse consulting companies, nursing homes, pharmaceutical companies, and clinics.

Any time you see a gap in service, a prevalent need, a fresh idea—that is where you go. Remember what Russell Simmons said: "There is a vast space of things that are not done."

HOT TRENDS

There are currently nine hot trends that will require nurse entrepreneurs:

1. Complicated, confusing health care systems plus chronic diseases plus an aging population add up to a need for case management. Of all of the hot trends, case management, life care planning, and nurse legal consulting are the absolute hottest. With the nation's new health care system fully under way, a nurse's role in overseeing patient care is only going to increase. As the complexity of care increases and the demand for accountability grows within new models of care, the role of the case manager is increasingly important. Case management and care coordination are seen as ways to fix some of the nation's health care problems, including high costs, uneven quality, and disappointing outcomes. Nurses are able to connect the dots for health care delivery—and our new role has already been proven highly effective. The American Nurses Association notes, "The value of nurses in care coordination roles has been demonstrated by a reduction in emergency department visits, decreases in medical costs and, most importantly, a significant increase in survival rates with fewer readmissions."[4] As the nurse case management role becomes more valued and visible, it will be in higher demand—specifically for those dealing with our aging population. Adults sixty-five years of age or older comprised 44.7 million in 2013 (the latest year for which data are available)—or 14.1 percent of the US population. But by 2060, this will skyrocket to 98 million older persons—more than double their number in 2013.[5] There has never been a better time to assist our aging community members with their health care (see chapter 6, "My Expertise," for more on that).

2. Aging baby boomers. The 77 million existing baby boomers (US citizens born between 1946 and 1964)[6] are currently in need of our services and will definitely need us in the future as their health and mobility decline. Their assets represent 70 percent of the total of US assets—and they are responsible for 50 percent of all discretionary spending.[7] Many elder care services require case managing skills (see chapter 6, "My Expertise," for more on that).

- **In-home care.** Thanks to the miracle of modern medicine, the elderly are now able to live independently, but frequently not without help. Of course we are talking about traditional in-home care for general or specific health concerns—but what about concierge services as part of that same service? Grocery shopping, chauffeuring, pet care, housekeeping, and the like can be bundled—saving the senior time and headaches.

- **Full-time in-home care.** Because of temporary or permanent illnesses and disabilities, part-time assistance may not be sufficient to allow the elderly to remain in their own homes. Sometimes round-the-clock skilled nursing care is required, and agencies that supply competent and honest help are—and will be—in great demand.

- **Visiting nurse / travel nurse.** Nurses who are trained for specific health issues can be literal lifesavers on a short-term basis. People with acute conditions may need a visiting nurse. Of these conditions, the most prevalent is heart disease, which accounts for one in four deaths in the United States,[8] followed by cancer, the second-leading cause of death,[9] and lower respiratory diseases, which end the lives of nearly 150,000 people a year.[10]

- **Estate planning, investment, life care planning, and advance care planning.** Helping boomers manage the life savings they collectively possess will provide plenty of work for legal, financial, and nursing professionals who assist them in creating life care and advance care plans (see chapter 6, "My Expertise," for more on that).

- **Personal improvement.** Long concerned with how they look and feel, boomers won't hesitate to spend retirement dollars on regimens and treatments that let them feel and look great. Entrepreneurs who effectively deliver services such as coaching, Pilates, yoga, nutritional counseling, and Botox—or other beauty treatments—will have a great market. Also, as mentioned before, boomers often love special retreats catered to overall wellness or specific health concerns, such as weight loss, diabetes, cardiac issues, skin care, mindfulness, and relaxation. If these services are offered through a clinic, it feels like a chore, but a separate getaway might sound like fun.

- **Retirement recreation.** One of the benefits of good health is the ability to remain active, and boomers will pursue vigorous activities in retirement as no generation before. Many of my baby boomer friends don't bother with traditional retirement activities of golfing and fishing—they are out there mountain biking, kite sailing, and snowboarding. Creating interesting outings that are staffed by medical professionals would be an incredible niche!

3. New technology and telemedicine. Patient portals, electronic communications between patients and health care professionals, and remote diagnostic equipment are all here to stay. The problem is that many people are frustrated and confused with the technology and need your assistance—or possibly your new innovative procedure or invention. Also, 70 million people in the United States are now using wearable tracking devices[11]—for everything from pulse rates to calories consumed. These technologies need to be effectively included in an overall health assessment and used by health care professionals when engaging with patients. Is anyone doing this well? Other growth in this field is technology training. For instance, simulations can be used for cardiac surgery training or in stations to give nurses practice with cases like septic shock or acute respiratory distress syndrome.[12] Another area of growth is telemedicine. Formerly relegated to rural health care, insurers are now seeing the benefits of telemedicine in widespread areas and populations—and are reimbursing these services.[13] And now that smartphones and tablets are the norm for communication, it's finally time act on this trend! A recent report projected that the number of consumers using home-health technologies will grow to 78.5 million by 2020, a number that could actually be conservative given the new incentives for "population health."[14] Tech-savvy nurses and telenurses to the rescue!

4. The epidemics of diabetes and obesity. The incidence of diabetes worldwide has quadrupled since 1980[15]—with an estimated 29.1 million afflicted in the United States alone (and nearly 28 percent of these cases are undiagnosed).[16] Plenty of adults, children, and specific communities will need your help in all areas—awareness, prevention, weight loss, education, training, transport, in-home visits, transplants, and wearable device installation and monitoring.

5. New regulations. Because of new regulations from the Centers for Medicare and Medicaid Services, the Affordable Care Act, and state regulatory bodies, more emphasis is placed on electronic records and prescriptions, compliance with protocol, performance improvement, and efficiency in services. As population health becomes an increasingly important part of health care reform, organizations will need help with data analysis, communicating and engaging with patients, and helping them to maneuver through health systems.[17] There now is a need for more consultants to assist with education, supervision, and reporting.[18, 19] This is where you come in! (See chapter 6, "My Expertise," for more on that.)

6. Changing cultural and geographical demographics. The United States has 150 different ethnic cultures with over 311 different languages spoken.[20] More people are immigrating to the United States, and more people are moving from rural and suburban areas to urban centers. Nurse entrepreneurs will help patients from different backgrounds navigate through an unfamiliar health care delivery system.

7. Staffing shortages. It is no surprise to any of us that health care is booming with a projected 26.5 percent growth rate, but did you know that by 2022 nearly one in eight jobs will be in the health care sector?[21] This is because of a change in age demographics and the increasing use of technology. Of course, nurses are perennially in demand, and most of us think that staffing agencies and recruiters will handle hiring for hospitals. But did you know that much of the job growth will be in nonhospital settings?[22, 23] Operating an independent staffing agency can involve RNs (who are the most in demand)[24] and other types of health care workers in a variety of settings.

8. Nurse practitioner opportunities. More and more states around the nation have passed laws to grant nurse practitioners independent prescriptive authority and full practice authority. This opens up many new opportunities for nurses to establish advanced direct-care businesses in the health care market.

9. Infections on the rise! Zika and Ebola outbreaks cause shudders of concern, and we all know that there plenty of other infectious viruses and bacteria that can wreak havoc on a school, health care facility, university, corporation, or community. Because of increased use of antibiotics and antibacterial agents and lack of protocol for hygiene, outside experts are often hired to assess risk, educate stakeholders, evaluate compliance with regulations, create interventions, and remediate for infectious diseases. Worldwide, infectious diseases are the leading cause of death in children and adolescents and one of the leading cause of death in adults,[25] and in the United States, infectious diseases are on the uptick.[26] However, bolder measures for prevention are now supported by the US Public Prevention Health Fund—which means that funding is available to support private and public entities' efforts through the Centers for Disease Control[27] and the Department of Health and Human Services.[28]

PROMISING SELF-EMPLOYMENT AND ENTREPRENEURIAL OPPORTUNITIES

Cardiac rehabilitation and electrophysiology nurses usually treat older adults with coronary artery diseases who are attempting to make changes in their lifestyles to avoid further complications after surgical or other major interventions. Some self-employment ideas for nurses with these specialties include facilitating retreats, workshops, or vacations that cater to healthy lifestyles and offer specialized education and support; presenting seminars and courses for the public on lifestyle changes, smoking cessation, or how-to sessions for electronic devices and apps (such as Fitbit or MapMyRun); operating fitness centers (alone or with other nurses) that include cardiac rehabilitation in a supportive environment; providing staff to cardiac rehab units in health care facilities; offering unique and helpful products (such as webcasts and YouTube videos, books, or workbooks); and consulting, training, or teaching at cardiac centers, fitness centers, and nonprofit organizations such as churches or senior centers. Currently in the United States, one in four people die from heart disease.[29] It is the leading cause of death. Furthermore, the US Administration on Aging reported a population of 44.7 million adults sixty-five years of age and older in 2013 (the latest year for which data are available), or 14.1 percent of the US population. By 2060, this number will skyrocket to 98 million older persons—more than double the number in 2013.[30] These patients will need our individualized care and support.

Health coach nurses bring people skills, health expertise, organizational skills, and energy to their patients. Health coach nurses (or lifestyle coaches, or wellness coaches) assist others in assessing their health and creating positive, targeted changes, especially for people with chronic ailments and individuals who are just trying to be more healthy and happy. Health coach nurses have the benefit of spending more time with patients and really getting to the heart of the matter. As a result, they may see real, concrete improvements. Health coach nurses become patients' champion, sounding board, expert listener, motivator, mirror, and accountability specialist! And you can customize your advice to fit each patient's needs. The end result is a patient who effectively manages his or her own personal health and life—very rewarding indeed!

Nurse consultants provide specialized services or advice. The good news is that nearly every aspect of health care delivery and the health care system benefits from the expertise of nurse consultants. Drawing upon your own specific experience and knowledge, you can objectively assess systems, procedures, people, services, publications, and products and make valuable recommendations, complete with timelines, goals, and follow-ups. I founded my own business-consulting and coaching company, Nursing Career Consultants, LLC, and let me tell you, helping other nurses reach their goals is incredibly rewarding! I provide Nursing Business Success Systems, training and speaking events for implementing the systems. If you'd like to learn more, please check my website, www.NursingCareerConsultants.com.

Diabetes/nephrology nurses can embrace a big market demand. As of 2016, 9.3 percent of the Americans have diabetes (27.8 percent of these people are undiagnosed).[31] Diabetes is nearing epidemic proportions. Nephrology nurses could consider being an independent contractor with health care facilities, renal dialysis centers, clinics, and home health agencies. These nurses could consider ownership and management of fixed or mobile dialysis units, staffing agencies that provide nephrology nurses to dialysis units and health care facilities, nursing continuing education seminars, public wellness programs and support groups, and product creation and sales.

Nurse educators are responsible for teaching student nurses and providing continuing education and training for practicing nurses. The level of education required depends on the educational setting. Oftentimes, real-life clinical experience trumps degrees or certificates. Self-employment options include tutoring; scholarly research; clinical research; scholarly writing; coaching writing; editing; independently consulting schools of nursing and health care facilities to provide education to staff members; designing or selling educational curriculum or products such as programs, textbooks, and educational tools; offering cardiopulmonary resuscitation (CPR), advanced cardiac life support (ACLS), or pediatric advanced life support (PALS) instruction, etc.

Emergency nurses thrive on the challenges and immediacy of the emergency room environment. However, a 2010 study in the *Journal of Emergency Nursing* indicated that approximately 82 percent of emergency nurses had moderate to high levels of burnout, and nearly 86 percent had moderate to high levels of compassion fatigue.[32] Their rich ER experience could be put to great use with self-employment and entrepreneurship!

Some options include: being an independent contractor with prehospital emergency medical services, working with health care facilities to provide emergency and high-risk transport services, and working with cruises, camps, and resorts—either in a caring capacity or as an educator, trainer, or consultant. Other opportunities include being an owner and operator of air and surface ambulance transport services; creating curriculum and continuing education courses for emergency nurses, medical technicians, paramedics, and 911 dispatchers and others; teaching classes for certification in ACLS, CPR, and PALS; training and certifying individuals in life support for other companies; owning and operating a staffing agency that provides nurses for camps, schools, and cruises; sales and after-the-sale programs for automatic external defibrillators; and emergency management consulting.

Forensic nurses combine clinical nursing practice with knowledge of law enforcement and provide direct care to victims. Like ER nurses, they experience high stress—but most love the challenge. They are involved in the investigation of abuse, assault, and accidental or unexplained death by collecting evidence and compiling reports. Self-employment options include being an independent contractor with law-enforcement agencies, correctional facilities, coroners' offices, medical examiners' offices, and insurance companies. Other opportunities include owning and operating private autopsy facilities, private investigation services, agencies providing correction nurses to prison facilities, or agencies providing nurse examiners to law enforcement.

Holistic and alternative care nurses have a great business opportunity. Holistic health and alternative medicine is a rapidly growing and increasingly accepted field of health care. If holistic and nontraditional care are used exclusively by a patient, it is considered alternative medicine. If alternative treatments are used alongside conventional medicine, it is called complementary.[33] In 2012, 33.2 percent of U.S. adults used complementary health approaches—and the trend is only growing.[34] Most holistic nurses are actually practicing integrative medicine—drawing from many sources and traditions to treat patients of all ages with acute or chronic illnesses or injuries. The care focuses on wellness from a spiritual and natural perspective. Care includes treating the whole person, not just the disease—and it includes preventive medicine. Integrative medicine is absolutely the future of medicine.[35] In fact, the National Institutes of Health set up five new research centers at a cost $35 million to study integrative approaches to wellness.[36]

Holistic and alternative practice includes aroma therapy, art therapy, Ayurveda services, colon hydro therapy, cranial sacral therapy, education, essential oils treatment, herbal and herbal medicine, ionic foot bath facilitation, massage therapy (see massage therapy nurse section below), master energy therapy, mindfulness coaching, natural health practitioning, reiki or energy healing, and being a movement specialist, including qigong, tai chi, and yoga. Other ideas are health-club owner, owner of holistic practice or retail business, owner of holistic resort, owner of a pain management center, product manufacturer or sales, seminar production and speaking, or yoga, tai chi, or qigong studio owner.

Infection-control nurses play a very important role. Infections are on the rise, and the United States is heavily funding prevention efforts with the new Prevention and Public Health Fund.[37] Infection-control nurses identify, track, and control infections in health care facilities, develop methods of prevention in health care facilities, implement immunization programs, and develop biological terrorist response protocols. Generally, no patient care is involved.

For a clever model of someone who is an infection control educator and prevention specialist, please see Nancy Haberstich's profile in this chapter. Some other ideas for self-employment include pre- and postregulatory survey consultations, consultations on nosocomial infection eradication and prevention, policy and procedure writing for health care facilities, and guideline and mandate writing for regulatory organizations and governmental agencies.

Informatics nurses identify, collect, process, and manage data and information to support nursing practice, administration, research, and the expansion of nursing knowledge. Informatics nursing is the combination of health care—and its need for information management—with information technology.

Self-employment opportunities include working as an independent contractor with health care facilities, computer and software businesses, educational institutions, regulatory agencies, research entities, medical libraries, and pharmaceutical companies or working in software and hardware sales, education and training, systems-management consulting, or data-analysis consulting.

Nurse inventors or innovators are the most creative. If you have ever thought that a process, form, system, device, computer program, or treatment could be improved, now is your time! If you think it is far-fetched to monetize your awesome idea, it isn't! Literally hundreds of nurses have created innovations that improved patient care, employees' health, environmental outcomes, and more! Please see profiles below of Amy Hickman, Dina Robinson, and Dan Tribastone. Please also see chapter 6 for how to get your idea to market.

Legal nurse consultants may or may not be licensed attorneys. They often serve health care organizations, private investigators, government agencies, insurance companies, corporations, law-enforcement officers, judges, law firms, and other legal entities by providing their medical expertise. They provide assistance to legal and insurance cases involving medical claims such as product liability, medical negligence, toxic torts, workers' compensation, and personal injury. They help stakeholders understand complex medical jargon and evaluate the claimant's medical condition in order to determine the legitimacy of the medical claim. They also assist in the procurement of expert reviews and evaluation of care, and they provide input into the claim-resolution strategy based on evaluations. They support managers with implementation of risk-management activities—all while trying to protect the assets of a corporation. They may also write litigation documents, conduct medical and legal research, analyze medical records, and assist with insurance claims investigations.

Legal nurse consultants are often self-employed and can be in high demand. Typical services that a legal nurse consultant might provide include the following:

▸ Independent research
▸ Educating attorneys regarding medical facts and issues relevant to the case
▸ Identifying standards of care, causation, and damage issues
▸ Conducting client interviews
▸ Providing initial case screening for merit

- ▸ Conducting research and summarizing medical literature
- ▸ Applying multidisciplinary standards of care and regulatory requirements
- ▸ Preparing chronologies of medical events and comparing and correlating them to the allegations
- ▸ Identifying and determining damages and related costs of services, including collaborating with economists in preparing a cost analysis for damages
- ▸ Assisting with depositions and trials, including developing and preparing exhibits
- ▸ Organizing medical records and other medically related litigation materials
- ▸ Locating and procuring demonstrative evidence
- ▸ Collaborating with attorneys in preparing or analyzing complaints, answers, and motions for summary judgment, interrogatories, deposition and trial outlines; queries for direct and cross examination; document production requests; and trial briefs, demand letters, and status reports
- ▸ Identifying and retaining expert witnesses
- ▸ Acting as a liaison among attorneys, physicians, and clients

Areas of practice include personal injury, product liability, medical negligence, elder law, toxic torts, workers' compensation, risk management, medical licensure investigation, fraud and abuse, compliance, criminal law, and other applicable cases.

Self-employment options include owning and operating an agency or independent legal nurse consultant providing consulting services to attorneys on a need-for-service basis; writing continuing education for legal nurse consultants; writing textbooks; and teaching legal-nurse consulting.

Massage therapy nurses (see also holistic and alternative care nurses above) can bring incredible insight, knowledge, and approaches to their daily practice, especially if they start their own therapeutic or medical massage clinic. A nurse-run clinic can attract a special niche market of clients who are seeking massage therapy as part of rehabilitation, chronic care, and pain management—not just for relaxation and stress relief. There is definitely a market for this! As of 2016, a full 56 percent of people have received a massage for soreness, stiffness, or spasms; to relieve or manage stress; for prevention or to improve quality of life; for injury recovery or rehabilitation; to keep fit or healthy and maintain wellness; or to control headaches or migraines.[38] A license from the state and credentialing from a national organization are required.

Staffing agency or recruiting agency nurse owners create a brighter future for nurses. "Nursing agency" is generally a term for a company that provides nursing staff to health care facilities. Some agencies serve as placement companies that recruit from foreign countries. Other agencies provide skilled in-home medical or nonmedical care for adults, seniors, and children.[39] The future is very bright! Any agency involved in recruiting, hiring, and staffing will be in great demand.[40] I won't go into great detail here because so much is involved with this kind of start-up. It is quite promising, given the current health care and demographic trends.

Occupational health consultants honor their responsibilities. If you perform occupational health assessments within a health care facility, you know how important this is! Routine physical assessments, educating workers about hazard control, providing vaccinations, and counseling on healthy lifestyles lead to increased productivity, employee retention, and job satisfaction. Becoming an independent consultant to local corporations and small businesses could be a rewarding role!

Pharmaceutical and medical sales nurses sell and promote pharmaceutical and medical products and services, and this often involves exhibiting at trade shows, traveling to facilities, and educating and training patients and clients after the sale. By 2020 there will be a huge shift in pharmaceutical marketing from a mass-market to a target-market approach to increase revenue,[41] so RNs may be able to rely on their specialized fields to help them reach the right consumers. Some ideas for self-employment are market and product sales; research, invention, design, or improvement of an existing medical service or product; manufacture or sales of a medical service or product; and Federal Drug Administration documentation writing.

Prenatal, perinatal, labor and delivery, midwifery, lactation, and postpartum nurses bring hope and knowledge to parents. It is a science and an art to care for and educate parents throughout pregnancy, labor, delivery, postpartum care, breastfeeding, and infant care. For those called to one or all of these areas, there is a great need for wise, calm, and nurturing individualized attention in the positions of doula, midwife, retreat facilitator, lactation consultant, personal educator for mothers and families, and birth coach. Exciting enough, a new trend is online birth coaching! Non-care options in this field are breast pump rentals, sales, and service; product invention and sales; in-home safety inspections for the new parent; education and advocacy; and owning and operating a birthing center.

Private duty or privately paid nurses enjoy their freedom and pay. Many of the specialties in this list mention the entrepreneurial idea of creating a staffing agency that employs nurses for private, in-home care for a variety of local patients (see "Nursing agency or staffing agency or recruiting agency owner" above for more information). However, some nurses work for individuals on a long-term, exclusive basis. These positions are acquired through word-of-mouth recommendations, marketing promotions, or recruitments through a nursing agency. Most are required to sign nondisclosure contracts and all must be discreet, as these patients—or their families—are oftentimes affluent, professional, and possibly famous. Some private-duty nurses are in hospitals to supervise the care of a client's loved one.

Research nurses work with all aspects of pharmaceutical, nursing, and medical research. Patient care can be involved when working with clinical research centers that monitor patients. Independent RN employment options include grant writing, data analysis, and being an independent contractor to pharmaceutical companies, research centers, universities, clinics, and health care facilities.

Sales and marketing nurses develop self-employment opportunities to sell products and services. These careers may include pharmaceutical or alternative product sales, on- or offline marketing, medical equipment sales, and sales and marketing management.

Senior health service nurse business owners provide quality care for elderly. Aside from the other services on this list that cater to seniors, nurses may want to create independent services for foot care, dementia care, companionship, medication management counseling and supervision, home-safety assessments and supply recommendations, workshops and retreat facilitation, private-duty nursing, and case management.

Telecommuting nurses and nurse practitioners are highly trained nurses who provide phone consultation, telemedicine, or appointment-based care for a variety of issues. These nurses use phones, tablets, smartphones, and computers to assess and treat patient injuries and mental disorders or illnesses, to educate patients about their conditions and provide feedback on potential treatments, to perform home-health assessments, to collaborate with medical staff and other patient-care providers, and to provide on-call care to patients at home or in the workplace. Some nurses have created nursing apps for certain populations. This is telecommuting nursing, but on a more immediate basis—and not necessarily for chronic or acute issues. You may consider creating your own app or working with an existing one.

Nurse writers and editors make their living by writing or editing in a variety of publications: popular magazines, trade magazines, scholarly publications, television shows, fictional books, or for their own blog. A professional nurse blogger or writer may write for a school, organization, or a large website. Such a writer may earn money from advertisers on her website or earn from writing for other blogs and publications.

Nurses who work as professional writers may be paid by the article, on an hourly basis, or under another agreed-upon arrangement. Being a freelance writer, editor, or blogger may sound like a dream business. Blogging alone is not profitable; however, professional bloggers may be able to match their personal/business goals with their content to get hired for writing deals or to promote or sell products and services. There are many nurse authors who create fiction or nonfiction books based on their everyday lives in health care.

A NOT-SO-EXHAUSTIVE LIST OF SELF-EMPLOYMENT, AT-HOME, AND START-UP IDEAS FOR NURSES

- Acupuncturist
- Addiction counselor
- ADHD coach
- Adult day care owner
- Advocate for patients and nurses
- Aero-medical or in-flight transportation service
- Agency or staffing service
- Allergy and environmental toxins consultant, industrial and residential services and educator
- Alternative medicine
- Anesthesia specialist
- App designer
- Aromatherapy
- Art therapist
- Arthritis and rheumatology services provider
- Artist
- Asthma consultant or educator
- Athletic competition event planning, supervision, consulting, and coaching
- Author
- Autoimmune disorder consultant, in-home care, and training
- Ayurvedic services
- Blogger
- Burn nurse and burn prevention
- Cardiac rehabilitation and electrophysiology provider
- Cardiopulmonary resuscitation educator
- Care management provider
- Case manager
- Chemotherapy nurse for in-home care, education, and training
- Childbirth educator
- Children's health speaker, educator, advocate, writer, or childcare consultant
- Clinical research services owner

- Coach
- Colon hydrotherapy provider
- Community organizer and community health nurse, working as a consultant or analyst
- Compliance consultant and accreditation consultant
- Concierge nurse
- Conflict resolution consultant
- Conflict resolution provider in health care settings
- Consultant
- Continuing education provider
- Cosmetics and skin-care services, sales, and marketing provider
- Craniosacral therapy provider
- Death investigator
- Dermatology and cosmetic services provider
- Developmental disabilities services provider
- Diabetes educator
- Diabetes home services provider
- Domestic violence center operator and nurse examiner
- Doula and perinatal nurse
- Eating disorders services provider
- Editor
- Educator
- Efficiency expert and consultant
- Elderly transition care and advocacy provider and liaison
- Emergency management consultant
- Ethicist
- Essential oils therapy
- Faith community or parish nurse
- First aid educator
- Food development consultant
- Forensic nurse
- Fraud and abuse investigation services provider
- Geriatric care manager
- Health and wellness coach

- Health care dispute analyst
- Health retreat organizer and facilitator
- Health policy analyst and lobbyist
- Health product distributor
- Health promotion and education provider
- Health writer and blogger
- Healthy cooking educator, writer, and retreat organizer
- Herbalist, herbal medicine provider
- Historian
- HIV/AIDS specialist; in-home services, advocacy, training provider; and writer
- Holistic life-change strategist and coach
- Holistic nursing provider
- Home health nurse services and staffing provider
- Hospice services, consulting, advocacy, training, and staffing provider
- Hyperbaric nurse
- Humorist
- Infant care and lactation services, in-home or advocacy provider
- Infection preventionist
- Informatics specialist
- In-home care service provider
- Inspirational speaker
- Integrative medicine specialist
- International health nurse
- Insurance and risk assessor
- Inventor
- Keynote speaker
- Learning and disability services, in home, advocacy, consulting, and education provider
- Legal consultant
- Lice treatment, removal, or education provider
- Life care planner
- Life coach
- Lobbyist
- Long-term care services provider

- Marketing and sales
- Massage therapy owner and educator
- Master energy therapist
- Media and news agency consultant
- Medical aesthetics for skincare, cosmetics, or salon services
- Medical bill auditing specialist
- Medical billing services provider
- Medical coding specialist
- Medical equipment salesperson
- Medical legal consultant
- Medical record auditing services provider
- Medical researcher
- Meditation and mindfulness coach
- Midwife or nurse midwife
- Missionary nurse (not really self-employment, but worth noting)
- Mother and baby nurse
- Movie-set nurse for first aid and advising
- Natural health practitioner
- Natural skin care specialist
- Neonatal home transition services provider
- Nephrology nursing provider
- Network marketing specialist
- Nonprofit organization director
- Nursing educator
- Nursing informatics specialist
- Nurse midwife
- Nursing videos producer
- Nurse staffing provider
- Nutrition consultant and support nurse
- Occupational and industrial health consultant
- Oncology services provider
- Organ donation education, advocacy, and support provider
- Pain management services provider

- Patient advocacy consulting, speaking, writing, concierge services provider, case manager
- Patient safety advocate, consultant, speaker, and writer
- Peace Corps volunteer (this is worth mentioning!)
- Performance improvement consultant
- Perinatal nurse or doula
- Perioperative and postoperative home-care services provider
- Pharmaceutical representative, salesperson, or consultant
- Pharmaceutical research nurse
- Podcast, webcast, or radio personality
- Policy development consultant—corporate, small business, or governmental
- Poet
- Postnatal, perinatal, prenatal care and support services provider
- Pregnancy care, support, education, writing, and prenatal, postnatal, and perinatal care and support services provider
- Prehospital emergency medical services
- Preventive health consultant, writer, blogger, and speaker
- Private-duty nurse
- Public policy adviser
- Public speaker
- Recruiter
- Reiki and energy healing specialist
- Rehabilitation nurse
- Researcher
- Respiratory home services provider
- Retreat organizer, promoter, and facilitator for health care providers, patients, or for preventive-care measures
- Risk-management consultant
- Salesperson and marketing specialist
- Scrubs design and sales specialist
- Seminar development and facilitation specialist
- Senior health services provider
- Sexual health educator
- Sick childcare provider for busy parents who can't stay home

- Space nurse and astronaut (okay, this one isn't entrepreneurial, but wouldn't it be awesome?)
- Speaker—public, small workshops, video blogs
- Spinal-cord injury services provider
- Sports nutrition consultant for retail, education, and retreats
- Staff development educator
- Staffing and agency services provider
- Stress management coach or consultant
- Surgical support nurse coach
- Telecommuting nurse practitioner
- Telehealth nurse
- Telephonic triage nurse
- Television show host
- Transcultural nurse
- Transportation services provider for critical care, elderly, dialysis, or flights
- Travel nurse or remote area nurse
- Traveling, transport, retrieval, emergency flight, or flight escort nurse
- Tutor, private
- Urology home services
- Utilization review
- Vascular treatment provider
- Weight-loss coach
- Wellness educator or coach
- Women's health services provider
- Wound, ostomy, continence home services provider
- Writer
- Yogi, yoga center owner or teacher, traveling yoga teacher

WE DID IT, SO CAN YOU

Dan Tribastone, an innovative nurse.[42] When you know your field inside and out, you have the perfect opportunity to create solutions to major problems that affect not only you but many others. Orthopedic operating room RN Dan Tribastone came up with an entrepreneurial opportunity out of sheer frustration in 1995. As many of you know, during orthopedic surgery, the body part undergoing reconstruction is constantly flushed with water. Tribastone noted: "The spent fluid was collected in small containers. An operation could produce 75 to 100 liters of fluid [which required 25 to 35 canisters]. Nurses were constantly having to disconnect and reconnect containers." The containers were connected to two lines—one to the hospital's vacuum line and the other to the drainage tube from the operating table. Nurses made anywhere between 150 to 200 new connections to the waste fluid connectors during every procedure.

Tribastone realized that they just needed to buy larger containers. But after extensive research, he realized that such a container wasn't available for purchase; it actually didn't exist. So, he explains, he eventually located a resource called the *Thomas Register of American Manufacturers* and requested samples from container manufacturers. "I got dozens of samples, most of which collapsed from the vacuum pressure. . . . But finally, I was able to find a steel container that held up. I added two connection ports and started to use them at work."

These new, larger containers proved to be very handy indeed—cutting the number of container changes by 80 percent. So Tribastone placed a tiny advertisement in the *Operating Room Nursing Journal*. After he received $1,000 in orders, he realized he was on to something. By 1997, his 3.5-gallon Omni Jug canister was selling for $25, and by 2001 Waterstone Medical's sales approached $5 million.

You see, Tribastone truly understood how customers would use the product because he was one of them. "Sales were a lot easier when customers realized that I came from the operating trenches," he explains. Tribastone notes, "Nurses immediately recognized I wasn't a smooth-talking salesman, but instead was really just one of them."

Amy Hickman, BSN,[43] recalls the constant frustration of untangling all the many tubes and lines on her little patients in the PICU at Children's Hospital in Omaha. At times, it could take up to 45 minutes to straighten the lines to ensure the proper medications were being administered. In her mind, she designed the perfect gadget but didn't have the slightest idea how to get started.

One day, while visiting her sister, she met her sister's neighbor, who just happened to own a plastics company. She told him about her idea, and he agreed to build a prototype. That was the beginning of the Hice Device (named after her sister because she introduced her to the neighbor). Today, the Hice Device is being used at Children's and is available to other hospitals for use through Frontier Medical Industries. "The

Hice Device helps nurses in many ways," said Hickman. "It helps them with time management, patient safety, and makes lines so much easier to identify."

Nancy Haberstich, RN, MS,[44, 45] invested her entire retirement into starting her clever business, Nanobugs. Referring to herself as an "infection preventionist," she brings her cartoon "Nanobugs" posters, books, T-shirts, smocks, games, smartphone apps, playing cards, and programs to schools and other institutions around the country to promote understanding of infections and infection prevention.

Nanobugs—which are adorable cartoon microbes—entertain and educate people of all ages about practical microbiology. "With emerging pathogens and the incidence of infection increasing rather than decreasing, it seemed to me that we needed a fresh approach to the issues surrounding infection prevention—compliance with hand hygiene and immunization," Haberstich said.

When asked how she came up with idea, she replied, "I had an old poster on my home office wall of cartoon microbes from a 25-year-old campaign from a drug company. My grandchildren were always interested in the microbe characters and their names. I decided that if they can learn the genus and species of dinosaurs, they could learn the scientific names of the microbes. Grandson Ted was interested in Pokémon cards, and I decided that I could make a card collection of the microbes that would interest children and teach their mothers."

But Haberstich didn't stop at children and schools. "Health professionals are never interested in the microbiology behind infection and control measures, and so I thought that a humorous approach might engage them." Look out for her new Academy of Clean—designed to reach and teach cleaning professionals and food safety workers!

Jean Aertker, NP,[46, 47] is the owner and nurse practitioner of Tampa Occupational Health Services, which provides employee health and wellness services. This specialty practice offers preplacement exams, DOT exams, OSHA and Hazmat surveillance exams, substance abuse and drug testing, independent medical exams, vaccinations, lab testing, and disability exams to small businesses and large corporations.

"It is a privilege to represent nursing through a business perspective," Jean says. Jean doesn't stop at running a successful business; she also is on the board of directors of the American Association of Nurse Practitioners' District 11.[48]

Dina Robinson, RN,[49, 50] and her sister Crystal—also an RN—noticed a need for an emergency body piercing-removal tool kit. "Folks chuckle when they hear this . . . but there is nothing humorous about it—removing piercings can be a real challenge and impede a person receiving health care in a timely manner," said Robinson, who works as an RN informaticist at Good Samaritan Hospital in Kearney, Nebraska. She continues: "Body piercings need to be removed for many reasons—nipple and belly rings can interfere with being defibrillated; a tongue piercing can keep someone from getting an oral airway; if a person needs an MRI, a surgical patient with a piercing can cause the grounded cauterizer to burn through the piercing. These are just a few examples, but there are many medical implications."

Robinson's sister, Crystal, was a correctional nurse having trouble removing body piercings from inmates. The sisters put their heads together and researched how medical professionals handled body piercings in an emergency situation and how correctional facilities handled the removal of body piercings. After one year of researching, they realized that nothing had been invented, so they needed to develop a body-piercing remover.

Once the SerRobCo (a combination of letters from three last names) device was designed and made, they were off to the market. Advertising and promoting to the correct market is important, and these nurse entrepreneurs traveled the country giving presentations and used the services of business consultants.

Since there is no other device like it, stories about SerRobCo appeared on ABC, CBS, and NBC and in the Associated Press. SerRobCo is now an international corporation selling emergency body piercing removal kits to health care, law enforcement, and penal institutions all over the world. The device is manufactured in Hong Kong and Pakistan.

Donna Schmidt, RN,[51, 52] decided to become an entrepreneur in addition to her busy career as a registered nurse in New Jersey. She knew all about colon hydrotherapy and ionic detox footbaths, the cornerstones of her new holistic health care business, because she had been a patient for so many years. Schmidt explains: "The colon is an important part of your health. It synthesizes vitamins, blocks pathogens," she explained. Keeping it clean is essential to well-being.

When her hydrotherapist moved out of state, leaving a void in the market, Schmidt seized the opportunity to marry her loves of nursing and holistic health. "I realized that as a nurse, I can make colon hydrotherapy a more value-enhanced service," Schmidt said. "I'm checking vital signs, making sure the client's lungs are clear, the heart is good, that there are positive bowel sounds, to ensure their safety." Thus, Cleansing Waters, LLC, was born.

While she was confident in the practice side of her new venture, what she didn't know was how to advertise and market these services to potential clients in her community. After reaching out to a mentorship program, she was able to devise a strategy to develop a powerful marketing system. Rather than hire a public relations firm, Schmidt approached businesses she frequented—such as Weight Watchers and a yoga studio—and got permission to leave info on her services. Paid ads were limited to specialized publications. She said: "If you break it down to where you think you'd derive the most benefit, you're not throwing money away." Any exposure—whether through social media, her constantly updated website or through local television spots—seems to garner more and more attention and excitement for her thriving business.

NURSE SOCIAL ENTREPRENEURSHIP: A NATURAL FIT FOR COMPASSIONATE PEOPLE

Social entrepreneurship is an approach that uses innovative ideas and practical models to achieve a social good. Some examples of this are Blake Mycoskie's TOMS Shoes, which donates a pair of shoes for every pair sold; Josh Nesbit's Medic Mobile, which allows health care workers to explain patients' symptoms—and transmit medical records—using text messages in remote areas of the world; and Jeff Mendelsohn's New Leaf Company, which sells environmentally responsible paper.

Social entrepreneurship is well suited to nurse entrepreneurs because of nurses' great sense of compassion. While most entrepreneurship companies are commonly viewed as business intended to achieve financial gain, in nursing, entrepreneurship could be viewed as seeking to achieve good health outcomes for the largest number of people. As such, these initiatives represent examples of nurses doing good for the larger society.

In contrast to the traditional business model of entrepreneurs, a social entrepreneur focuses on creating social returns. Thus the main aim of social entrepreneurship is to further social and environmental goals. Although social entrepreneurs are most commonly associated with the voluntary and not-for-profit sectors, these businesses need not exclude making a profit.

Taking the social entrepreneurship approach in health reform places nurses on a common platform with people who have noticed a need and developed a way of remedying the issue.

SNAPSHOTS OF SUCCESS

- **Alice Sable-Hunt**, MBA, RN,[53] founded Sables Foods in 2006. This food-product company creates nutrition bars designed for the cancer community. A year later, she founded the Edwards-Hunt Group, a life-science consulting firm that helps disease-specific nonprofit organizations. The Edwards-Hunt Group uses a vanguard model, a "bench to bedside" approach to develop drugs that form a direct link between the laboratory and the patient's bedside.

- **Holly Gale**, RN,[54, 55] worked as a registered nurse for twelve years but took a leave of absence to care for her ailing father who suffered from pancreatic cancer. Years later, she took another leave to care for her ailing mother—also diagnosed with cancer. These profound experiences prompted her to start her own business to serve those in need, and she launched First Light Home Care in September 2011. The comprehensive services include companion care, dementia care, travel companionship, respite care, and rehabilitation. There are now franchises all over the country.[56]

- **David Martin**, RN,[57, 58] a nurse since 1980, founded VeinInnovations, a vein health and treatment company in the Atlanta area. Since 2002 it has grown to a staff of thirty-five and three locations.

Chapter Six

My Expertise: Case Management, Legal Nurse Consulting, and Life Care Planning

MY JOURNEY

I REFRESHED WHAT I HAD learned about community nursing when I decided to build and grow the life plan elder law business with my husband, David, an estate planning and elder law attorney. I had studied some theories, policies, and practices, but it was sink or swim at the beginning to apply them to my daily practice. What really helped me was my guiding principle: I aimed for the best possible outcome, medically, physically, financially, mentally, and psychosocially, for each of our clients. And I treated each one as if they were my parent—which kept me plowing through policies, talking on the phone with insurance companies and all related parties, and poring over forms and data analysis. When you will settle at nothing less than the best outcome for the people you care about, you will learn just about everything there is to know!

You might think that you need all kinds of special certifications—all kinds of letters behind your name—to become a case manager, but there is nothing like experiential learning, especially since each client, patient, and case is unique! In the end, I believe you can rely on your nursing experience, existing credentials, sheer determination, and desire to help others in case management.

Building and providing case-management services for the elderly and chronically ill or seriously injured clients is the most interesting and challenging journey I've ever had. I called on every ounce of energy and skill I had for problem solving, communication, management, and patience to create the best outcomes for our clients. In this complex and confusing health care delivery system, I would work in a constant mode of creative problem solving—making the impossible possible for people who otherwise would be completely lost and forgotten in the system. It is so rewarding. When we draw on our nursing skills and critical thinking skills, we are the true leaders in patient care.

Right now, so many elderly and chronically ill or seriously injured patients feel helpless about their current issues and hopeless about their future. There is nothing more gratifying than fully assessing their physical, mental, financial, medical, and psychosocial lifestyle data to create a concrete, meaningful, clear, viable, plan that secures their future. My hope is that this is what attracts you to case management, care management, life care planning, and advance care planning: creating the best possible life now and in the future for countless people who truly need your assistance.

You will be surprised how many people are not prepared at all to handle the legal, medical, and financial consequences of a chronic or serious illness, a severe injury, or disability. For nearly a decade, working with many attorneys and other medical or financial professionals, I helped thousands of clients define, prioritize, and manage every aspect of their care to optimize quality of life and independence, such as how to:

- ▸ Secure optimal care at home or in facilities;
- ▸ Identify issues created by the high cost of care;
- ▸ Define public and private financial sources to help pay for long-term care;
- ▸ Organize advance care plans to help make decisions ahead of time in the event of incapacitation, such as DNR (do not resuscitate), ICD (implantable cardioverter-defibrillator) or ventilator use, tube feeding, palliative care, etc.
- ▸ Obtain right choices to achieve peace of mind.

An effective life care and advance care plan is critical to secure quality of life for those who suffer from chronic illness, such as Alzheimer's, multiple sclerosis, cardiac or diabetic problems, kidney failure, stroke, cancer, catastrophic injury, etc.

WHAT IS CASE MANAGEMENT ANYWAY?

The Case Management Society of America defines the work as follows: "Case management is a collaborative process of assessment, planning, facilitation, care coordination, evaluation, and advocacy for options and services to meet an individual's and family's comprehensive health needs through communication and available resource to promote quality cost-effective outcomes."[1] We need to be strong advocates, excellent communicators, and knowledgeable about a myriad of resources. We strive for cost-effective and optimal interventions and outcomes. Our goals are to center services around the patient, foster self-managed care, and keep patients out of the hospital. Most case managers specialize in geriatrics, rehabilitation, long-term planning after catastrophic illness or injuries, cancer, or chronic diseases. Some case managers work in pediatrics. An independent case manager can be remunerated by insurance companies, the public sector, or privately.

A case manager (also known as a care manager or sometimes nurse health educator) is the go-to person in a patient's life. As a case manager, you are dealing with physical, medical, financial, psychosocial, and mental needs by working with health care providers, family members, insurance companies, and community support resources—which means that you are dealing with their whole life support system. We make sure that patients get what they need, when they need it, for the best value. The case manager is the patient's lifeline for their entire well-being.

Over the past century, case management has meant better-coordinated care for patients with complicated health needs. Since the 1990s we have transitioned our role from being very small and specific to being an essential tool in managing complex cases in workers' compensation, behavioral health, insurance, and managed-care organizations. Today, tens of thousands of case managers are employed in a range of health care settings and in independent practice. Case management is among the job categories projected to grow much faster than average in other occupations.[2]

MAKING THE IMPOSSIBLE POSSIBLE

Not long ago, during our family vacation, we were having a snack and drinks in a hotel lounge, exhausted after a day of walking and sightseeing. Colin, my eight-year-old son, had brought a little Lego kit to play with while we relaxed. After a few minutes of playing he came to us with great frustration in his voice: he had lost the tiny toy gun from this, his favorite set.

We started hunting for the teeny-tiny, gray plastic piece. We searched under tables, between seat cushions, behind curtains, and all over the lounge. We found a little bag of cereal under a couch, an orange that had rolled behind the curtains, and even another toy, but we couldn't find his tiny Lego toy gun.

We finally gave up and explained to Colin that this little object was camouflaged in the carpet, and it was simply impossible to find. He would just have to deal with his loss or remain frustrated. But Colin didn't give up. He continued to comb the area for another hour. Suddenly he ran up to us: he had found the toy gun, and he was over the moon! I hugged him tightly and said, "Colin, you have made the impossible possible!"

The type of focus, purpose, and persistence that Colin showed is not unlike case management. We don't stop working, searching for solutions, and trying to fit all of the pieces of the client's puzzle together, and usually we have made what seemed impossible possible. The good news is there is always a best solution in which the end result is a win-win-win, and this makes nurse case management a most desirable and rewarding journey.

A NOT UNUSUAL REWARDING CASE

Here is an example of the moving parts of a case all coming together. Four siblings once approached us regarding the future of their eighty-year-old mother. She had just lost her husband and was still living independently in her home. Because she suffered from diabetes, congestive heart failure, and a myriad of other issues, the children had made accommodations to her home (such as moving her bed to the main floor and retrofitting a bathroom) and hired a visiting nurse and housekeepers. However, they worried that even with all of this, she was still not able to properly care for herself. Additionally, her bank account had dwindled quickly, and they were concerned not only for her health but that they wouldn't be able to sustain the costs of her living independently.

The first thing we did was to conduct a thorough, objective assessment. We spoke with all the members of her family about their worries and goals. Interestingly, one of the siblings wasn't participating in their mom's care; she had a different viewpoint than the other three. We took that into consideration. Then we visited their mother's home, met with her, and conducted a safety assessment. We then compiled her health history and insurance and financial data.

After looking at all of the physicians' diagnoses, orders, and medications, we compared them and noticed that different specialists were not talking to each other. Furthermore, after speaking with her, we realized that she wasn't taking her medications correctly. She—and the family—didn't know any better. Her physicians were contacted for more integration of services and orders. A case review like this is especially important during a time of transition to another level of care.

Since she was rapidly declining in health, which we gathered from her health data, from our assessment with her, and from observing her struggle to breathe and walk, we came up with a care plan that included a recommendation to move her to an assisted living facility. The facility the children found was willing to accept her, so they signed a 12-month contract and paid a total amount of $10,000 up front as a deposit. It looked like the short-term goal was met: she was safe and taken care of. But we realized that they still couldn't sustain the costs in the long run. This time, we visited her in the assisted living facility, prepared with all our findings, and met with the staff of the facility. As we expected, we were able to develop a workable life care plan involving a coordination of her insurance policies, financial assets, and medical needs, as well as her and her family's wishes. We were able to create a sustainable, affordable plan that ensured her care for many years to come.

Here is the thing: there are many stakeholders in this process. The private insurance company, the care providers, the hospital, the Department of Human Services, the facility, the patient, and the family—all of these parties may have different ideas about what is the correct path. Emotions, prior knowledge, rules, contracts, and money can all play a part. However, it is up to you as the independent case manager or your case-management company to navigate these waters and chart a smooth course. And sometimes it may look like a seemingly impossible case, but if you have a clear system and logical way to run your business, even the seemingly impossible cases can work out really well, which is the true value and reward of this journey.

WHAT IT TAKES

Case managers, over the course of care, work in seven major areas of activity:[3]

- ▶ Case-management concepts
- ▶ Principles of practice
- ▶ Health care management and delivery
- ▶ Health care reimbursement
- ▶ Psychosocial aspects of care
- ▶ Rehabilitation
- ▶ Professional development and advancement

The core competencies and skills required are:

▸ Being well-versed in all aspects of care—including both financial and clinical elements

▸ Strong knowledge base of community resources and governmental procedures

▸ Communicating well with all stakeholders: patients, family members, legal teams, and health care professionals

▸ Excellent management, teaching, negotiating, advocacy, and research skills

▸ Ability to work well with interdisciplinary groups

▸ Ability to focus intensely on patients' and families' needs

▸ Ability to be an angel with patients and hard-nosed advocate on their behalf

SUBGROUPS OF CASE MANAGEMENT

- **Case managers** work toward getting clients to the appropriate services within their network.

- **Nurse life care planners** formulate a care plan for the life of the patient using financial codes to determine future money needed to care for the claimant's disability—usually after a catastrophic accident or illness. Working with insurance companies, attorneys, and others to develop a life care plan, independent nurse life care planners determine the future needs, services, and costs of care for the patient over their lifetime.

- **Rehabilitation nurses** assist the patient to get as well as possible and reduce the costs associated with recovery and other needs related to the disability.

- **Workers' compensation nurses** help patients get back to work and guide them in managing their own health in order to lessen the effects of the disability and increase clients' functioning.

- **Elder care managers** work with seniors to ensure that they are provided with services that keep them active and healthy for as long as possible. Many independent elder care managers work with elder trust attorneys or families who do not live near the patient.

- **Nurse paralegals** work with attorneys to offer legal services as well as working with health care issues.

- **Medicare set-aside consultants** create a financial document, a concrete plan forecasting the projected medical needs of the client throughout his or her life. These plans are used to determine insurance settlement figures and to create separate, untouchable funds to use after age sixty-five. Medicare requires that funds be set aside for future care under certain circumstances.

SELF-EMPLOYMENT OPTIONS

▶ Independent private consulting

▶ Staffing service that provides consultants to law firms and insurance companies

▶ Agency providing managed-care case managers to health care facilities, managed-care organizations, and insurance companies

▶ Consulting companies for legal firms, financial services, insurance companies, employers, or individual clients

TRENDS IN CASE MANAGEMENT

The 2009 Commission for Case Manager Certification's "Role and Functions Survey" identified the following key trends for case management:[4]

▶ Increased visibility and accountability in case management

▶ Government playing a greater role in regulatory compliance

▶ Increased focus on return-on-investment and cost-effectiveness value

▶ Increased caseloads and work-load limitation, meaning that case managers must do more with less

▶ Blending of roles or the need to know more about anything and everything

▶ Increased need for advocacy and balancing of competing interests

▶ More activity in wellness, prevention, and chronic-disease management

▶ Greater emphasis on client-centered care, including cultural sensitivity, the psychosocial aspects, and the medical home

▶ Greater emphasis on transitions of care and collaboration across care settings or continuity of care

▶ More evidence-based care

▶ More use of technology in case management, such as electronic health records, predictive modeling tools, Internet-based education and communication tools

MAKING THE INVISIBLE VISIBLE

Like bamboo shoots after rain.—Chinese proverb

Number one on the aforementioned list of case-management trends is increased visibility and accountability. People need to actually know that case managers exist and know what we do. I once went to a speaking engagement featuring Catherine Mullahy, the author of *The Case Manager's Handbook.*[5] She said in her speech that even her husband doesn't know what she does.

I know that many patients think of case managers as "that nice lady who comes to visit and talk to me about how I'm doing," and many health care providers are grateful, but they are sometimes confused and wary of case managers' work. The good news is that the public knows now that we exist and that we can be hired privately to evaluate, coordinate, and advocate on patients' behalf. The trend points toward more awareness, understanding, and promotion of our services.

Dr. Suneel Dhand said: "Without the case manager, the job of any hospital physician is impossible. So whether you next speak with them at random times during the day, or at organized multidisciplinary rounds, take a moment to appreciate the awesome work that they do to keep our patients moving."[6] Nurse case managers bring great value of objectivity, health care expertise, client services, and cost-effective benefits to insurance companies, law firms, and many other patient care organizations as well. We certainly need to build on this positive trend of understanding, acceptance, and acclaim by actively promoting awareness of our professional presence.

And with complicated health care systems, changing demographics, and more chronic diseases, now is truly the best time for nurse entrepreneurs to get in the business or expand your current business! And get your G.A.M.E. plan started with the following four easy steps:

1. Generating Vision for Leading
2. Accessing the Field
3. Monitoring It All
4. Empowering the Most Engaged Players

The four steps of the G.A.M.E. plan will be described in detail in chapter 8, 9, 10, and 11.

Part 3:

PLAY THE GAME WELL

Chapter Seven

Deep Awareness, a Limitless Sky, and a Smile on My Face

WUKONG

A person without a smiling face must not open a shop.
—Chinese proverb

This is how I view the world—and it has served me very well:

- The universe is abundant and limitless.
- Everything we think can be achieved.
- There is no such thing as luck; we make our own luck through hard work and dedication.
- Working hard toward goals with great determination and focus are excellent habits of a successful person, but the work should be playful, freeing, and fun—and the focused mind should actually be relaxed and rested to accomplish its goals.
- Be self-aware and follow your instincts—which are influenced by both direct experience and indirect learning.
- Keep your eyes on the big picture and don't sweat the small stuff.
- All challenges and crises are actually opportunities.

In other words, have a Monkey King mind-set. Monkey King's very name in Chinese, *Sun Wukong*, derives from *wu*, awareness or deep understanding, and *kong*, sky or air. Sun is his surname. It means having that deep consciousness of both the self and of the limitless universe, which like the sky and air, never ends. There is truly nothing that cannot be achieved if we can conceive it. I have seen it time and time again in my life: when I set my intention to succeed, I do. The sky's the limit! But here is the thing: *Sun Wukong* doesn't work at his accomplishments; he plays his way to success. If your work doesn't feel like joy, you are probably doing the wrong work.

INSIDE THE MONKEY KING MIND

Know yourself and you will win all battles.—Sun Tzu, *The Art of War*

The process of starting and running a business should feel liberating, invigorating, and challenging—your attitude is, how can I solve this new, interesting puzzle? Being my own boss is a divine exercise of creativity and ingenuity. There are interesting solutions to every problem, fascinating people with whom to engage, and fast-moving curveballs to be hit out of the park. When I sit down to work on particularly daunting problems such as sticky employee issues, legal wrangling, or facility breakdowns, I approach it with an attitude of "what interesting thing has been given to me today?" If I am bogged down with feelings of worry and frustration, it isn't work, it's torture. Like Monkey King, I think of what fun tool will I use today? How will I get out of this jam?

When we are playing, we are learning, we are growing, and we are building. Italian physician, educator, and philosopher Maria Montessori was a pioneer in understanding how children learn and develop. She posited that children's work is their play and their play is their work; it is how we grow and understand.[1] I learned about this philosophy when I enrolled my son in a Montessori children's house. I have come to believe that this is the same for adults. When we are given the freedom to select our own activities and pursuits and then engage in them uninterruptedly and without outside pressures, it opens up passions, curiosity, and creativity. It feels like child's play, but we are accomplishing so much more!

Don't get me wrong. I work hard. I didn't create the successful businesses by just wishing, dreaming, and playing. I get up every morning and research, talk with clients, write, plan, and study, but when the energy I expend is for the goal of creating a business that helps others, creates financial stability and freedom for my family, and positively impacts thousands of lives in the long run, it feels absolutely effortless. Even the big roadblocks feel like teachable moments on the field rather than injuries that sideline me. This peaceful, prosperous, balanced life is worth the effort.

And now I shall say something about focus and determination. Yes, I am very focused. My inner compass is always pointing in the direction of success, but I don't focus to the point of excluding all joys from my life. I don't fixate on minute issues for hours. I find that to be counterproductive. The Chinese idiom *wu ji bi fan* means things turn into their opposites when they reach the extreme. When you are hyperfocused on solving a problem, accomplishing a goal, learning a new task, or working on a project, you get the opposite effect—you lose all sense of perspective, creativity, curiosity, and playfulness that would come with a relaxed mind.

The renowned educator Barbara Oakley calls this state of mind "diffuse."[2] She says that while you obviously have to focus your cognitive energies in order to learn something (or write something, read something, or memorize something), that's only part of what is happening. She notes that in the focused mode we channel our thinking to a specific task or problem, and this thinking takes place in the brain's prefrontal cortex.[3] The diffuse mode is a less focused style of thinking where different areas of the brain link up to form a big-picture view of a problem. This mode of viewing a problem can help to unblock us if we can't see creative alternatives. Have you ever been in the shower reflecting on the day or driving home from the office and a solution to a problem that you weren't thinking about sprung into your mind? That's diffuse mode in action! Studies have shown that we often switch back and forth between the two modes during our day-to-day activities.

Oakley recommends that you avoid being extremely driven and work-obsessed or procrastinating. Instead you can pace yourself with the Pomodoro Technique:[4, 5] First decide on the task to be done (see my tips about how to create an effective to-do list), then set a timer for twenty-five minutes. Work on the task until the timer goes off, and if a distracting thought pops into your head, just write it down and go back to the task at hand. After each timer goes off, put a checkmark on a piece of paper and take a short break of three to five minutes. As soon as you have four checkmarks, take a longer break of fifteen to thirty minutes; then go to back to the first step of selecting a task. Repeat this process steadily over days and weeks.

It turns out that many great thinkers such as Thomas Edison, Charles Dickens, and Salvador Dali took breaks to meditate, walk, nap, or do chores so that great thoughts would come to them![6] Remember *wu ji bi fan:* avoid the extremes and all good will happen. Work to the extreme and you will get the opposite effect!

LILY'S TIPS FOR MAINTAINING A PLAYFUL AND OPEN MIND

- If you think about something before a break or nap you have a better chance of **dreaming** about that thing. You could try what Dali did. He would put a ring of keys in the palm of his hand and relax in a chair; when the keys fell to the floor, the sound would wake him up, and he would immediately begin work on the creative thought that came from a relaxed and open mind.

- **Exercise** is a wonderful way to gain entry into the diffused mode of thinking. It is beneficial in many ways beyond the obvious physical ones. Those benefits include the generation of new neural pathways, encouragement of healthy growth hormones, and the reduction of depression and anxiety.

- **Sleep** is like a dishwasher that cleans out toxins in the brain. Some people think that you should live on four hours of sleep to run a business, but what kind of business will you create with a tired, stressed, toxic brain?

- **Tune out.** I personally do not let the technology in the office or home distract me. While I enjoy listening to calming jazz music as I work, I don't toggle over to the Internet, I don't answer the phone unless it's an emergency or scheduled appointment, and even in my down time, I don't watch much television or play video and computer games. Having a calm, uncluttered mind serves me well. Of course I have fun playing board games and volleyball and socializing; I'm just talking about those black holes of technology that can suck up so much of your time and mental acuity.

LILY'S TIPS FOR MAINTAINING
A PLAYFUL AND OPEN MIND

- Since childhood, **meditation** has been a part of my daily routine. There is nothing more malleable than the human mind, and I find it so beneficial to just settle it down for a while and allow it time to heal and rest. More and more we hear of successful CEOs who practice some form of meditation because it slows down the day, makes life richer and fuller, and encourages more meaningful interactions with others. I learned meditation from my nai nai, my father's mother. She lost her parents during the communist revolution. She married my ye ye, my father's father, who owned successful mines, but those were taken away. All of their possessions were gone or destroyed, and she was left to support the family with embroidery. You might think that she would be nervous, unfocused, or depressed for her entire life. But she was not. She had a calm mind, a gentle way about her. She taught me the benefits of calming one's mind to enhance one's entire life.

- **Commit to an everyday practice.** Schedule self-care—including breaks to do nothing. Set alarm reminders to breathe deeply and cater to what the body needs, display positive thoughts, dance around, convert should into could, and burn a candle or diffuse essential oils. I personally light a fragrant yet calming candle at the beginning of every day.

- Enthusiastically and unapologetically **give yourself permission to take time for self-care.** We nurses are so accustomed to putting others' needs first. We don't realize that we need to be healthy and well first before we can serve others and our own business—otherwise we burn out. The last thing I want is for you to replace one stressful job with another!

If you feel like you could never approach something like running a business with a playful and relaxed attitude, just try it for twenty hours! Josh Kauffman famously wrote that all you need is twenty hours, or forty minutes a day for a month, to learn something new.[7]

I would advise that you make a list of the target behaviors, such as meditation, sleep, or avoiding Pinterest, and attitudes, such as playfulness and cultivating a relaxed mind, and work on your most difficult challenge first. It can be fun if you see it as a new game, and if you reward yourself afterward--Oh, and one more tip about being playful: I always reward myself when I accomplish a goal. What will be your reward for accomplishing your first goal?

THE INNER VOICE, THE *ZHIJUE*, THE SIXTH SENSE

When a monk asked, "What is the dao?" The master replied,
"Walk on."—Daoist saying.

Zhijue is the Chinese word for instinct. Business guru Napoleon Hill called it the sixth sense.[8] It is your connection to God, Intelligence, or the Universe. As I have developed as a nurse and entrepreneur over the past twenty-eight years, I have gained experiences and confidence to follow my *zhijue*. It is challenging to describe because it is a feeling and awareness. I have developed the habit of not overthinking things to the extent that I extinguish the flame of the idea. It seems workable to me that when I hire people, make decisions about the direction of the business, create marketing plans, and find business partners, I follow my inner voice.

Of course, I don't follow my *zhijue* to the extreme—like a feather floating around aimlessly in the wind. I don't constantly make entirely uninformed decisions. Remember *wu ji bi fan*—things going to the extreme create the opposite effect? Well, the antidote to *wu ji bi fan* is *zhong yong*—avoiding extremes; achieving balance. I'll touch more on this concept of staying centered in the next chapter regarding leadership, but suffice it to say that it is because of my developed inner voice, or *zhijue*, and self-awareness, or *wu*, that I know if I am making an extreme decision or not. So when, like the monk, I want to know *the way*, I say to myself: "Walk on."

I know this is pretty deep and unbelievable stuff. But it's the stuff that dreams are made of!

PICKING UP SESAMES

One drops a watermelon only to pick up a sesame seed.—Chinese proverb

Being an entrepreneur is the most humbling experience I have ever encountered. Yes, I approach my position with the confidence of a Monkey King, a trust in my instincts, and a faith in the eternal abundance, or *kong*, but through self-reflection and deep awareness, or *wu*, of my faults and limitations, I accept that I can't do everything and I'm not great at everything. I have a growth mind-set, and through daily practices of meditation, writing, and just plain thinking, I'm aware when my motivations have shifted, my emotions are aroused, or my ego is afflicted. When I get caught up in some conflict or another, I remind myself of an ancient saying, *Diuxigua jian zima*: "One drops a watermelon only to pick up a sesame seed." What this means is that when you get caught up in something small like a personal grievance, power play, or daily conflicts, you lose the big reward. It's all about keeping perspective. I try not to worry about the little sesame seeds. There are far too many trivialities and petty issues lying around—and when we stoop to pick one up, we stand up with very little to show.

To obsess about some perceived slight or oversight is just a waste of energy. Yes, be aware of the problem. Yes, learn. Yes, grow. But hold on to that big watermelon! Now I even have my friends using this phrase! Just last week, my friend said about her mother, "Oh, she's just picking up sesame seeds!" That made me smile.

SEE CHALLENGES AS OPPORTUNITIES

Be careful what you water your dreams with. Water them with worry and fear and you will produce weeds that choke the life from your dream. Water them with optimism and solutions and you will cultivate success. Always be on the lookout for ways to turn a problem into an opportunity for success. Always be on the lookout for ways to nurture your dream.—Lao Tzu

We are only human. The minute that there is a sudden change or an unforeseen problem, we may say, "Oh what now?" And after that initial shock, we need to center ourselves and remember the ancient Chinese proverb, "A crisis is an opportunity riding a dangerous wind." In a time of trouble, there is an opportunity to accept a challenge, learn something new, and become triumphant. In fact, we entrepreneurs should take stock of all of the things we complain about, all of those things that are broken in the system, and ask ourselves, are we up for the opportunity?

A QUICK TIP FOR PLAYING THE GAME: MAKE A TO-DO LIST THAT WORKS FOR YOU

When many people make to-do lists they write some major goals at the bottom and then put the easy, smaller tasks at the top. This makes people feel that they are getting so much done because they can cross off the little things, but recent research from psychologists and neurologists say that the correct method is to put the toughest and biggest goal at the top of the list and then break that goal into a manageable, specific plan that you can measure.[9]

So, for writing this book, I wrote down the chapter I wanted to write, listed the ideas I wanted to cover, and put down the number of pages that I planned to write in a day. I did the easy tasks—like formatting the font—toward the end of the day when I'm not as fresh. The idea here is that you are putting your real goals ahead of your minor tasks. If you don't put Start My Successful Entrepreneurial Business at the top of the list, you will be doing laundry instead.

So that's how I play the game internally. That's how I coach myself to be playful, keep a relaxed mind, not take petty things too seriously, follow my instincts, and see challenges as opportunities. My, *and your*, entrepreneurial business, is a game to be *played well* with practice, planning, teamwork, communication, cultivation of talent, critical thinking, creativity, curiosity, and managing risks—and all of this takes the insight of the kind of leader you can become.

Follow my four easy and solid steps of the G.A.M.E. plan, and see how well you can play.

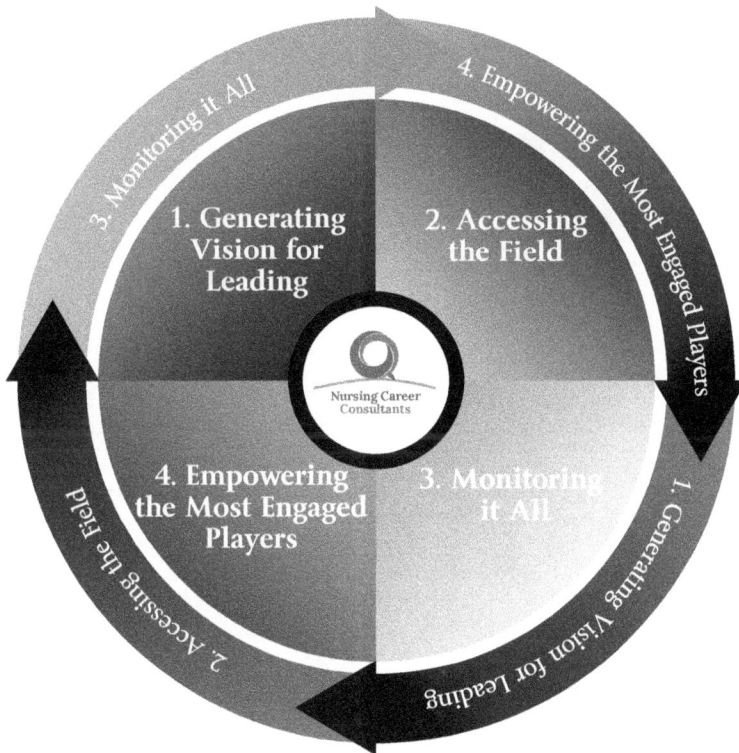

1. Generating Vision for Leading
2. Accessing the Field
3. Monitoring It All
4. Empowering the Most Engaged Players

Chapter Eight

Game Plan Step No.1: Generating Vision for Leading

DEVELOPING *WU*, DEVELOPING YOU

....

Know yourself and you will win all battles.

—Sun Tzu, The Art of War
....

ENTREPRENEURIAL NURSES TEND TO SHARE characteristics such as patience, compassion, integrity, and vision, which serve them quite well in leadership roles. Good leadership demands emotional strengths and behavioral characteristics that can draw deeply on a leader's mental and spiritual reserve—and we nurses know how to fire on all cylinders of intellect, faith, energy, and personal strength.

You know, I've heard it said a hundred times that leaders are born, not made. But I don't believe in this fixed mind-set; anyone can cultivate the necessary qualities through the processes I identify in the preceding chapters: self-reflecting or *wu*, meditating, cultivating balance and centeredness or *zhong yong*, caring for yourself, following your *zhijue* or instincts, thinking big picture, and working hard.

Before you begin your business, you must first use those strategies to develop your core—and I don't mean abs. An important aspect of leadership is that you must have a guiding philosophy or a fundamental purpose by which you lead your employees, develop your market plan, and sell your products or services. But if you don't know yourself and your core values, and you don't remain centered and balanced; you are a tree without roots and are destined to fall over.

This is how you build your business:

▸ Cultivate your sense of self, your *wu*—which leads to your core vision
▸ Then cultivate your business with great care and *zhong yong*
▸ Then positively impact the community and world

So first you must concentrate on yourself! You need a solid foundation within your very heart, soul, and mind! When you have self-awareness, or *wu*, and a vision statement, you can achieve clarity in your purpose. When you are a tall tree, you can see everything around you so clearly that you can grow and branch out. And, yes, you will be getting the most wind, but you will have deep roots made up of your core value, vision, self-awareness, and balance, and you will be able to bend with the wind, as you are resilient. You will be getting all of the sun, too. The most sun will shine on you!

Things will get confusing and demanding, especially in the health care system, but when you are deeply planted in your core vision and core values and have a sense of balance, you will be utterly rooted in your self-awareness, and you will not topple over.

Relying on luck, skepticism, and reactionary decisions ultimately leads to a loss of control and a dead end of no productivity and growth. Here is an old fairytale from my childhood that illustrates a lack of self-awareness and balance.

THE TALE OF THE MAGIC CASK

Once there was a man who found—buried deep in his field—a giant, earthenware cask. He dragged the cask home and his wife cleaned it. But, when the wife started brushing the inside of the cask, the cask suddenly began to fill with brushes. No matter how many were taken out, others kept on taking their place. "What great fortune!" said the man. So he sold the brushes, and the family lived quite comfortably on this enterprise.

One day a coin was accidentally dropped into the cask. Immediately the brushes disappeared, and the cask began to fill itself with money. Now the family was rich—for they could take out as much money as they wanted and it always refilled itself!

The man had an elderly grandfather who lived with them. He was feeble and afflicted with palsy—and there wasn't much he could do any longer—so the man set the grandfather to work shoveling out money all day. When the old man grew weary and couldn't continue, the man yelled at him in rage, telling him he was lazy and worthless.

One day, the grandfather's strength gave out. He collapsed into the cask and died. At once, the coins disappeared, and the whole cask began to fill itself with dead grandfathers! The man had to pull them all out and give them all proper burials, which used up all of the remaining fortune. When he was through, the cask broke, and he was as poor as before.

What is to be learned? The man lost his sense of values. As his fortune increased, he forgot what truly mattered and abandoned his senses and his core values; he went to the extreme. This could happen to any of us. When we are in the throes of something stressful, we can lose who we are. I see this in corporate health care; we are so busy with efficiency and billing and regulations that we forget that the patients are at the center of it all. And being entrepreneurs, we can get all tied up with bottom lines, minutiae, and putting out fires, and we forget what we are doing it for. This lack of core vision spills onto the employees, products, services, and ultimately the community and world. So ask yourself: Who am I? What do I value? What is my vision? And stick to that. When a positive or negative stimulus, such as a dropped deal, a big profitable deal, an angry customer, or a huge development happens, just remember your vision, your core, and stay balanced. Otherwise you may be burying dead grandfathers and losing your fortune!

OUR STORY OF *WU* AND *ZHONG YONG*

A family in harmony will prosper in everything.—*Chinese proverb*

At the beginning stage of building our life plan elder law business, we created a Saturday morning radio show on a local station that catered to an over-fifty and affluent demographic. David would give tips for estate planning, retirement, and elder life planning and field questions from callers. At first, the show was called *Life Happens*, but I advised that it should be called *The David Carrier Show* instead—which made great sense, as it would be getting his name on the tips of everyone's tongues. David has a delightful, humorous, and accessible personality, so it wound up being a highly rated program. Not only was it successful in attracting clients for the business, it was a profit-maker for the radio station. We were approached to create a syndicated program much like *The Dave Ramsey Show*.

We sat down and discussed all of the possibilities: nationally syndicated daily shows, traveling seminars, and cross-promotional products. But in the end, we landed back at the core values and the vision and mission of the business. Did we really want to forgo directly working with so many families in a meaningful way? Did we really want to be on the road and leave our small son behind? No. To follow some other path with this new golden opportunity wasn't being true to our core competency. We realized that the core value path was the right way. The business has since grown to a forty-person interdisciplinary team and has four offices in Michigan, with new offices set to open in Chicago soon.

SHINY OBJECTS

See the big picture, and don't get distracted by small
opportunities.—*Confucius*

I've seen a similar situation with my clients. We sometimes have an opportunity placed at our feet, and we don't know if we should seize it or not. Sometimes these shiny objects can be just distractions; sometimes they are true paths to success.

A good example of this is Dharmesh Shah, founder and chief technical officer of HubSpot. After creating a successful software company and growing to $10 million in revenue, he thought, "Hey, I've got a team in place, the company doesn't really need me, and I'm sort of bored and want to do something new. So, he made the big mistake of being a 'parallel entrepreneur.' Trying to head up two different startups at the same time. This was a huge mistake at many different levels. Turns out, startups are an all-consuming thing. You can't be all-consumed by two companies at the same time—it just doesn't work."[1]

New York Times best-selling author Tim Ferriss has this to say about "committing to too many 'cool' opportunities and projects. If you're not 100 percent excited, it should be a decline. 'Kinda cool' will fill up your calendar and leave you wondering where the last year—or ten—went."[2]

Entrepreneurs typically have an instinct for smelling opportunity, but that same killer instinct can quickly turn to weakness when it becomes a distraction from primary goals and core values.

So what are your core values? What is truly important to you? Is it your spiritual, mental, and physical well-being? Is it using your talents to their greatest potential? Is it being socially responsible? Is it honesty and integrity? Is it ease and simplicity? Is it being sustainable? Is it being connected with family needs? Meditate on these and write them down.

Once you have created a statement of your solid vision and core values, nothing can fundamentally shift you and your relationship to the world around you. Whether it is shiny new opportunities, office drama, new competition, customer woes, or marketing snafus, when you have consolidated everything about you and are centered and uniquely excellent, all things will swirl around you—but you will know exactly who you are. Most people will see what's on the surface—the strong tree—but won't know who the real you is, all of the deep and solid roots. As long as you stay centered and mindful of your vision, all sorts of difficult decisions and unexpected things will happen, and you won't be shaken. Remember, two-thirds of an iceberg lies below the water.

SURPRISING LEADERSHIP QUALITIES

To govern by virtue, let us compare it to the North Star: It stays in its place, while the myriad stars wait upon it.—Confucius

So as you cultivate a strong inner core, create balance in your life, and develop your instincts using the aforementioned time-honored processes, you must think of the other personal qualities you wish to attain to become a leader. Renowned Harvard psychologist Daniel Goleman claims that the most important quality a leader should possess isn't knowledge, charisma, eloquence, boldness, or IQ. It is the emotional quotient or emotional intelligence that makes an effective leader. Emotional intelligence is the "capacity of individuals to recognize their own, and other people's emotions, to discriminate between different feelings and label them appropriately, and to use emotional information to guide thinking and behavior."[3] Goleman believes that IQ only accounts for 20 percent of your success; the other 80 percent is determined by emotional intelligence. [4]

THE FIVE ELEMENTS OF EQ

1. **Self-awareness.** The following definition differs slightly from the ancient sense of *wu*, but it is basically the same principle that the ancient philosophers believed was essential to success as a person and leader. Daniel Goleman defines self-awareness as "The ability to recognize and understand personal moods and emotions and drives, as well as their effect on others. Hallmarks of self-awareness include self-confidence, realistic self-assessment, and a self-deprecating sense of humor. Self-awareness depends on one's ability to monitor one's own emotional state and to correctly identify and name one's emotions."[5]

2. **Self-regulation.** "The ability to control or redirect disruptive impulses and moods, and the propensity to suspend judgment and to think before acting. Hallmarks include trustworthiness and integrity; comfort with ambiguity; and openness to change."[6] This also is similar to *wu* in that you are developed in your sense of self to the extent that change, stimuli, and emotions do not make you bend and break in the wind. Leadership expert Ronald Heifetz also talks about this trait in being competent with "adaptive leadership."[7]

3. **Internal motivation.** As I mentioned in chapter 3, we need to be motivated by higher purposes than extrinsic rewards. Goleman defines this aspect of EQ as "A passion to work for internal reasons that go beyond money and status, which are external rewards, such as an inner vision of what is important in life, a joy in doing something, curiosity in learning,

a flow that comes with being immersed in an activity. A propensity to pursue goals with energy and persistence. Hallmarks include a strong drive to achieve, optimism even in the face of failure, and organizational commitment."[8]

4. **Empathy.** Goleman defines this as "The ability to understand the emotional makeup of other people. A skill in treating people according to their emotional reactions. Hallmarks include expertise in building and retaining talent, cross-cultural sensitivity, and service to clients and customers."[9] It is important to note that empathy does not necessarily mean compassion. Empathy can be used for compassionate or cruel behavior. That being said, leaders who are compassionate tend to attract followers and build more stable and profitable businesses. Some examples are Craig Jelinek, CEO of Costco; Jack Welch, former CEO of GM; Oprah Winfrey, CEO of OWN/Harpo Studios; Jeff Weiner, CEO of LinkedIn; and Howard Schultz, CEO of Starbucks. It is well known that compassionate entrepreneurship is the wave of the future.[10, 11]

5. **Social skills.** This skill set is a logical part of success, but it is often overlooked when people are looking to lead! Goleman defines this aspect of EQ as "Proficiency in managing relationships and building networks and an ability to find common ground and build rapport. Hallmarks of social skills include effectiveness in leading change, persuasiveness, and expertise building and leading teams."[12]

So, in addition to defining your core values, you may want to consider developing your emotional intelligence. You may wonder how to attain those attributes. I'm sure you won't be surprised by my answer: the same way you develop anything else, by developing your *wu* with meditation, self-reflection, awareness, and mindfulness. For instance, how do you learn how to become an acute listener and compassionate leader? By being in the moment, being mindful, and actually listening empathetically to others. When you are rushing around, totally inside your head, reacting to stimuli, and otherwise spinning, you are not maintaining your vision, you are not being measured, you are not being calm, and you are not leading. How do you develop your social skills if you are "picking up the sesames" and not centered, calmly understanding what's really going on, maintaining a sense of perspective, and deciding how to effectively react?

ANCIENT CHINESE LEADERSHIP QUALITIES

A leader is best when people barely know he exists; when his work is done, his aim fulfilled, they will say: we did it ourselves.—Lao Tzu

I came across a scholarly article from New York University comparing the leadership styles of the various Chinese leaders in history. These are the styles of what they called transformational leaders over China's 3,500-year history:[13]

- ▶ They identify themselves as change agents.
- ▶ They are courageous individuals.
- ▶ They value people's talents.
- ▶ They are value driven.
- ▶ They are lifelong learners.
- ▶ They have the ability to deal with complexity, ambiguity, and uncertainty.
- ▶ They believe in leading by example, not through force.
- ▶ They are visionaries.

All of these attributes ring true today, and I will cover each of these aspects in the following pages.

A closed mind is like a closed book, just a block of wood.—Chinese proverb

In my beautiful hometown of Guilin, there is a wildly popular tour boat adventure down the scenic Li River. As you round a bend you can see far off in the distance the Nine Horses Cliff. The tour guide will ask you, "What do you see?" From such a distance, only the most astute eye can make out a vague outline of the nine horses etched into the cliffs. They seem to be drinking, galloping, lying around, and frolicking. Legend has it that Monkey King came down from heaven and brought his nine horses, but when they arrived the beautiful Li River, the horses did not want to leave and they ran into the cliff and never came out again. So they are etched in the colored minerals and limestone for eternity.

Most people in the tour boats don't immediately see the nine horses, so they wait to come closer, but they still can't discern them. Then they travel even closer and can't detect them, and finally the boat approaches the sides of the white cliffs, but it is too late. If they didn't have the vision miles away, they certainly won't when they are brushing the sides of the limestone.

Legend says that if a person can point out all the nine horses on the precipice, she or he will be the winner of the next Imperial Examination. It is reported that Premier Zhou Enlai and some world leaders were able to recognize and identify all nine horses with ease. What does this say about vision?

Just like your inner vision, the vision—or goal—for the future of your business must be distinct and clear in your mind's eye. Others may not see it like you do—but an effective leader can help others see the vision as well. More importantly, a true leader will not let his/her ego get in the way with thoughts like "You all must do what I said!" An effective leader will gather the insights from research and from consultants, employees, and even competitors in order to see the vision more clearly! Remember *wu ji bi fan*: going to the extreme will get the opposite effect.

So what is your business's vision? It doesn't need to be complicated. It could be "to provide reliable, safe, and patient-centered care through innovative and efficient care-delivery models" or "to create technology that will advance health care practice."

Some sample vision statements are

1. Oxfam: "Our vision is a just world without poverty. We want a world where people are valued and treated equally, enjoy their rights as full citizens, and can influence decisions affecting their lives."[14]
2. Ikea: "To create a better everyday life for many people."[15]
3. Amazon: "To be earth's most customer-centric company; to build a place where people can come to find and discover anything they might want to buy online."[16]
4. Harley Davidson: "To fulfill dreams through the experiences of motorcycling."[17]
5. Hilton: "To fill the earth with the light and warmth of hospitality."[18]
6. Under Armour: "Empower Athletes Everywhere."[19]
7. CVS Caremark: "To improve the quality of human life."[20]
8. Kraft Foods: "To make today delicious."[21]
9. Toys "R" Us: "To put joy in kids' hearts and a smile on parents' faces."[22]

When the vision, or fundamental purpose for existence, is set, refined, well defined, and shared by all, it is time to write it down and make it the guiding principle for laying the foundation for building everything else in your business: strategy, management, operational activities, and pretty much everything else that happens in an organization. It is like sending the roots of awareness down deep. The tree of your business may bend, but not break.

ON A SUICIDE MISSION?

Failing to plan is planning to fail.—Chinese proverb

After you have defined your vision, you must create a mission statement. A vision statement is the statement of overarching goal, or reason for existence, while a mission statement provides an overview of the group's plans to realize that vision by identifying the service areas, target audience, and values and goals of the organization.

It doesn't matter the size, age, or type of business—all elements need to have a single, harmonious foundation. Executives, managers, staff, patients or clients, suppliers, and stakeholders need solid philosophical principles, or a frame of reference, on which to base their expectations, decisions, and actions. It helps set the tone—and reason—for everything, including branding, marketing, hiring, training, promotions, communications, purchases, and investments.

When I think of establishing a mission, I think about a fairytale from my childhood.

A long time ago a farmer was plowing his fields when suddenly a hare rushed across in a great hurry, crashed into a stump, and immediately broke its neck. It died right there.

"What good luck!" the farmer said, picking up the dead hare. "If I can harvest hares like this one, I can make a much easier living. Why shouldn't I just wait here instead of toiling all day long, sweating blood, tiring my body out, like a great fool?"

Thinking this a great plan for success, the farmer no longer worked. He would sit by the stump, his hands supporting his cheeks, waiting patiently for more hares.

Unfortunately, no more long-eared and short-tailed food came. Day in and day out the farmer starved, only to become the laughingstock of the neighborhood.

What do I mean by sharing this story? Well, it's simple: the farmer's vision was actually a positive and clear one, to provide food for himself. But his mission was impractical and devoid of some serious critical thinking skills—one component of which is to be able to think logically about the consequences of a plan—to understand the statistics of probability. Another important skill that would have served him well would have been collaboration or soliciting input. If he had gathered other farmers to share his plan, they would have seen the error in his judgment. Sometimes we can be blind when we create our mission statements.

The mission statement of my consulting and coaching business, Nursing Career Consultants, is "To help you build your business that is joyful to run and that generates more income in a simple, effective and powerful way. We achieve our mission through interpreting the success secret and distilling it into actionable easy-to-use intelligence." Notice how the foundations of our mission are simple, yet profound. We want you to be prosperous and happy. Certainly these are both attainable and measurable outcomes! Also, notice it is we, not I. Collaboration on the mission is of utmost importance. As entrepreneur guru, Napoleon Hill, once said, "You must have the advantage of the experience, education, native ability, and imagination of other minds."[23]

Facebook's mission is quite clear: "Our mission is to make the world more open and connected. As we grow as a company we have five strong values that guide the way we work and the decisions we make each day to help achieve our mission."[24] The values, you could say, are their guiding principles—or vision—and they are: "Be Bold.

Focus on Impact. Move Fast. Be Open and Build Social Value."[25] So drawing on their vision and mission, all employees can plan accordingly. If someone were to come up with a new social media feature, they might ask the team: "Does this build social value?" "Can we create it quickly?" "Is this a bold or tepid move?" "Am I closed off to a better idea?" and "Would this positively impact our company and other's lives?" Your mission and vision should provide just that kind of value compass for your employees and yourself. I know that when we are working with clients, the end game isn't just giving them profitable ideas; it's also asking if they are finding joy in the process. That is our mission, to help our clients find balance and fun and be like a Monkey King, unlocking hidden potential all the way to reclaim the respect, freedom, and prosperity they deserve!

DECISIONS, DECISIONS

Leadership requires adaptability combined with boldness.—Chinese proverb

It is sometimes excruciating for me to make decisions, but I rely on my ancient wisdom, experience, and instincts to forge ahead.

Here are my basic beliefs about decision making:

1. Procrastination and indecision are the enemies of progress.
2. No creative process can begin until a decision is made.
3. Research well; make lists of pros and cons; weigh options.
4. The first instinct is usually correct.
5. To build up uncertainty undermines your plans.
6. Mistakes can be forgiven.
7. Focus on the present moment.
8. Be able to make uncomfortable decisions and take uncomfortable actions.
9. Make decisions promptly with the confidence and your core values.

In one sense, being mindful and present slows down time; it feels as if time is abundant, and there is all the time in the world. And truly time is the gift that is completely free from the universe. However, I agree with Napoleon Hill that "Life is a checkerboard, and the player opposite you is time. If you hesitate before moving, or neglect to move promptly, your men will be wiped off the board by time. You are playing against a partner who will not tolerate indecision!"[26] This is so true! Like Facebook, which includes in its mission to "be bold" and "move fast," I believe that leaders must be decisive and take bold risks in order to have the greatest impact, and we should be prepared to take on the consequences of our decisions.

TREES THAT BEND BUT DON'T BREAK

When the wind of change blows, some people build walls, others build windmills.—Chinese proverb

I find that Americans tend to think of leaders as rigid and fixed, like stalwart captains on the sea saying "Full steam ahead!" But I find that being an entrepreneur and a leader is a lot like being a nurse in that we must be able to be resilient and dynamic.

Ronald Heifetz agrees: "Leadership is the process of mobilizing progress—fostering people's adaptive capacities to tackle tough problems and thrive. . . . Changing environments and new dreams demand new strategies and capacities and the leadership to mobilize them."[27] We must remain nimble and flexible. Both our employees and we ourselves must be able to steer around obstacles and get back up when we fall.

I remember that when I first started developing the strategies to build the life plan elder law practice, I discussed the new vision of growth and services with the two employees. One of the employees seemed amenable and excited about the changes, but the other employee seemed threatened by changes to the type of small business in which she had an idea of how things should be done. The prospect of an unknown, possibly tumultuous future was frightening to her. After our initial conversation, she believed that we had threatened her with being fired, which of course wasn't true. I initially wept and fretted over this situation, but then I turned inward to my core. What she said and did wouldn't shift my core values.

This tree didn't break.

I had to be resilient in my emotions and responses and not overreact to this setback and negativity. I had to be dynamic and think differently about the situation. I took a step back and thought calmly and responded appropriately and steered around this obstacle. As I mentioned before, you must develop *wu* to hold steady in times of strife. Indeed, Heifetz mentions "holding steady" in *The Practice of Adaptive Leadership* as "withholding your perspective, not primarily for self-protecting, but to define the right moment to communicate. Also, remaining steadfast, tolerating the heat and pushback of people who resist dealing with the issue."[28]

I worked hard to bring all new employees into the fold, letting them know up front that we are a dynamic and growing workplace. I expect all team members to be resilient: we may change buildings (which we did); we may hire many more employees (which we did); we may open branch offices (which we did); and we may add more procedures and protocol (which we did). I like to say, "Preparation is not from the air; it's from the resilience." The only thing we can count on is change. So why not prepare for the setbacks and strife with a Monkey King mind-set of openness, joy, and a willingness to take on challenges?

Confidence in a leader is one thing, but the ability to be open to change and new ideas, and being able to get back up when one falls, is the greatest modeling of leadership of all.

START AT THE END

Be careful to think about the end at the beginning.—Chinese proverb

Critical thinking in the Western tradition means objective analysis and evaluation of an issue in order to form a judgment. This, of course, is an important skill for leaders. Through objective analysis of people, processes, products, and information, we can make connections, find solutions, and come to conclusions. It's important to not fall victim to irrational thinking!

And I've spoken so much about how important it is to think positively, creatively, diffusely, playfully, deliberately, compassionately, and with curiosity. These are important thinking skills for all leaders, especially nurse entrepreneurs.

I've also extolled the virtues of following your instinct and not just your intellect. And just to be clear, I don't mean just following your heart! I mean following your *sixth sense*—your *zhijue*, which comes from both your experiences and intelligence, direct and indirect, as well as from your connection to a higher source. This, too, is very important for leaders.

But now I'd like to talk about another way to view your entrepreneurial leadership skills, by beginning at the end. This is where you think of the goal and work backward from there, asking yourself along the way if the means will result in the desired end. This actually takes imaginative thinking, not necessarily critically thinking. Oftentimes

I see people who Just Do It! They do it, and then what? I see the big and little mistakes entrepreneurs make.

Sometimes we don't think from the end and plan backwards. We don't think of the consequences of our actions, how things will look, or how things will be experienced on the part of our clients, patients, and customers.

I've seen my consulting clients think of a clever strategy for their business, and then it winds up missing the mark. What seemed like such a good idea really may not be a sound idea. Please, take time to imagine what the actually process will look like and what the end result might look like. Think through the eyes of your patients and clients. Think of where they are in space and time, how they might be spending their time, what their values and lifestyle might be like, how they might perceive a marketing message, receive a service, or use a product. Using your imagination in this way not only helps with planning and decision making, it helps with setting an intention, so the universe knows your goal. The same goes for leading employees, creating products, and improving processes. Start with the end.

Again, this goes back to knowing yourself deeply, being mindful and aware, and using your instincts—but also it means using your critical thinking skills, in whatever form they may serve you.

GOAL!

Victorious warriors win first and then go to war, while defeated warriors go to war first and then seek to win.—Sun Tzu, The Art of War

As a leader, your main priority is to get the job done, whatever the job is. Leaders make things happen by:

▸ Knowing your objectives and having a plan of how to achieve them
▸ Building a team committed to achieving the objectives
▸ Helping each team member to give his or her best efforts

I will speak more about teamwork and monitoring progress in chapter 11, so for now, let's focus on goals so you can be proactive rather than reactive. If you fail to plan, you should plan to fail. Set a solid course, and it will all run smoothly. The following is my process for setting goals.

LILY'S LEADERSHIP GOAL-SETTING PROCESS

1. What are your own core values?
2. What is the vision and mission of your company?
3. What is the best strategy for accomplishing that mission? (Remember, begin at the end!)
4. What are your personal goals for the future, consistent with strategy and mission?
5. What are the overall goals for all—or part—of your business? Is it building, improving, growing, or even ending an aspect of the business?
6. What are your overall goals for the community and world? (Remember, first self, then business, then community/world. We are all interconnected and you don't get something without giving something!)
7. What are the overall goals for your team, and for each member of the team? Get input from all!
8. Goals can be about things that are achieved (e.g., dollar amount in sales by the end of 2016) or about the process of achieving them (e.g., building morale in the workplace and having fewer employee sick days).
9. Quantify and specify all goals. Don't be vague. So, instead of saying "increase client base," say something like, "attract three more ideal clients a week."
10. Make sure that all goals are measurable. (For example, "successful" is a vague, relative term. "One hundred" is measurable, and employee wellness, for instance can be measured by sick days and inventory surveys).
11. Decide on a long-term goal and a short-term goal.
12. Sequence your goals logically as you prioritize them.
13. Create a specific action item list and prioritize and sequence actions logically. (By specific: "interview four web designers" rather than "find a web designer.")
14. Decide who will do the tasks.
15. Create a viable, reasonable timeline for each task.
16. Create benchmark deadlines and desired outcomes for each task.
17. Write everything down in a prominent place where all can see.
18. Refer to goals at the top of the day—always start with the most difficult action item.

Your personal values and personal goals as well as your impact on the community should play a part in setting a goal for your business. As a leader in your own venture, you must be on board with all facets of the goals. If they don't align with your core values and future plans, or with how you connect with others, there will be great discord, and it will be less likely that you will be successful. This is part of *zhong yong*. When you are just self-absorbed with your own goals to the extreme, you are losing your balance. Think of everyone else when setting goals: your loved ones, your clients, patients, your team members, your community, and the world. With this balanced approach you will have great success—and more importantly, great harmony.

LILY'S TIPS FOR SETTING GOALS

- Goals must be measurable in time, money, otherwise quantifiable.
- Goals must be framed in time, with clear beginning and ending points.
- Goals must be accepted and recognized as important by everyone who will have to implement them.
- Everyone should get on board with the consensus that the most difficult goals or action items should come first.
- Keep the goals prominently displayed in your daily workplace. Think of creative ways to do this such as key reminder words, a clever phrase, or even a poster.
- The process is just as important as the goal.
- Both the process and the end achievement should be supported by rewards. Remember Carol Dweck's growth mind-set ideas: praise effort, not fixed traits.
- Keep the motto "Done is better than perfect."
- They should be realistic goals, challenging, but achievable. Do not change timelines if at all possible. If timelines must be changed, reconvene the entire group to rework the plan and discover what was unreasonable about the timeline and what were the unforeseen setbacks.

The last point is particularly important. Goals should give you and your team something to reach for. But they should not be unreachable, and their attainment or lack of attainment should not be dependent on a host of circumstances beyond a person's control.

BE PROACTIVE AND RESILIENT

The superior person, when resting in safety, does not forget that danger may come.—Confucius

We can try to manage risks by forecasting and evaluating the risks, by identifying some ventures we should embrace and some we should avoid. I know that risk management works!

SIX PIECES OF ADVICE, MINUS ONE

- *Ju an si wei*: think of danger in times of safety. When you are happy and things are going smoothly, it is time to think of how to improve, grow, and reevaluate goals, markets, and priorities. It is all part of being resilient and proactive—rather than stuck in the mud and reactive.

- Stay up on trends and new insights. Continue to partake in conferences, read books and periodicals, talk to colleagues, and be a part of community discussions and efforts, such as volunteering, writing articles, attending conferences, retreats, or meeting.

- If there is a setback or mistake that costs you resources, remember that the world is abundant. You may have lost your time, but you have gained new wisdom.

- When you fail, don't be shamed by the laugher of others. Everyone fails at some point. Whether we choose to get back up after we fall makes the difference.

- I don't really believe in luck, but I do believe *Danan bu si, bi you houfu,* which means: "After surviving a great disaster, one is bound to have great fortune." Which reminds me of something that happened to me when I was a child.

LILY'S GREAT FALL

Back during the Chinese Cultural Revolution in the early 1970s, adults were mandated by the government to read and memorize the teachings of Chairman Mao Tse-tung, and so they needed time to study together after the workday was done. One night my fuqin (father) *and my muqin* (mother) *were hosting the study group. Since I was only three years old, I fell asleep upstairs, and I usually slept through the night without any problems. But that night, I woke up and probably heard people chatting downstairs, and I was curious to hear more. And I probably climbed up to the second-story window to better hear their conversation, when suddenly I lost my bearings and fell out of the window and plummeted to the alley below!*

Through the window, fuqin's friend saw a shadow suddenly fall in the darkness, and they all heard a thud in the bushes. Fuqin's friend exclaimed, "That must be a cat that jumped from such a height!"

My muqin replied, "We have no cat!" and all the people ran out into the alley to the sound of my wailing.

There was little light, but my fuqin felt around the little four-by-four patch of flowers and shrubs to find me, gently picked me up, and held my wet body against his. I was damp, you see, not from bleeding as my parents feared, but from the urine released in fear. Unbelievably, I was completely fine. Not even one single bruise or scratch. They looked up at the eave and noticed a shred of my nightdress stuck on a protruding nail.

Fuqin and muqin looked at my torn dress and said to me, "Oh, our little girl, you are so lucky. Not only did the nail break your fall, you managed to land on a perfectly sized patch of soft earth for your little body! You didn't land on the brick pavement right next to it!"

Fuqin's friend then turned to him and said, "Ah, she is also very lucky because after surviving a great disaster, one is bound to have great fortune." Which is the old saying, "Danan bu si, bi you houfu." And they were right: that was the last of my tragedies. (My muqin told me that the first one was that I almost had to be born at home, as all the hospitals closed their doors to prevent further harm from cultural revolution battles in the city; The second one was that I was almost shot by a bullet when I was two years old, when my nai nai [grandma] *and I were sitting in front of her house and saw a bullet go through an iron basin right next to me.) Ha! I have been fortunate ever since.*

Perhaps you don't believe this. Perhaps it seems far-fetched that after a tragedy or setback will come great fortune. Well, I can point to hundreds of people who fell financially and were able to rebound spectacularly. Just off the top of my head, I think of those like Martha Stewart, Donald Trump, Dave Ramsey, and Steve Jobs—and corporations like Apple, Ford, Chrysler, and FedEx.

I truly don't believe in luck. We make our own luck, and when we believe that we will have smooth sailing ahead, we generally will. And even if we don't—even if we fail—we can stand back up, dust ourselves off, and continue. I think of the saying from the great Chinese philosopher and general Wang Yang-ming: "The great virtue of man lies in his ability to correct his mistakes and continually to make a new man of himself."

Yes, think of danger in times of peace and work to prepare for the future, but in the end, failing isn't so awful! With great risk comes great reward!

THE SIXTH PIECE OF ADVICE REGARDING FEAR

Okay. Fear is a biggie in entrepreneurship and leadership—and requires its own specific attention. We all experience fear, but the key is to notice it for what it is, feel it thoroughly, then forge on. I know this is easier said than done, but try to see it like this:

▸ Fear is information that what you are doing is spectacular. It is a gift of insight that what you are attempting is somehow uncomfortable or unusual, and it may end in failure somehow. Thank the fear for this information.

▸ Note that everyone feels fear and that fear is there to stop those who aren't as courageous—who don't want something badly.

▸ Holding onto fear is wasted energy and a poison that spoils what you are creating.

▸ We can't control the future. The only thing we can control is our own mind. So release the fear and attach your mind to a positive outcome.

▸ Trust in your vision, trust others, and trust in an abundant universe. Hold this faith inside you with the conviction that the positive outcome has been achieved. And it will be.

This idea of fear reminds me of another childhood tale.

BUYING SHOES

Once there was a man who wanted to buy a pair of shoes. He cleverly and carefully measured his feet with a piece of straw by making marks on it. Then he walked to town to visit the shoe shop.

Unfortunately, he was forgetful and left his piece of marked straw at home. So when he got to the shoe shop without the measurements of his feet, he was at a loss. Finally he thought of a solution and said to the shopkeeper, "I am afraid you'll have to wait until I fetch my straw."

He hurried all the way home, snatched the straw, and ran back into town. But when he reached the shop, night had fallen, and the shop was closed. Others heard about this and went to ask him, "Didn't you have your feet with you when you were in the shop?"

"Yes, of course," the man answered with perfect assurance, "But the straw was very carefully measured, and I am afraid my feet are not that trustworthy."

Do you see how this man is, adding fear to processes that needn't be fearful. He is failing to rely on his own critical thinking skills, and he is failing to trust himself (or at least his feet!). We would never be that foolish, correct? I have seen people who are afraid of moving ahead toward the life they dreamed of. They forget that they have earned degrees and have experiences; they forget all the problems they've solved, people they've helped, and wisdom they've acquired. When you have the right mindset, you will be confident that all will go well. The next time you have fear, say: "I've got this!"

TELL IT LIKE IT IS

Lead by personal example as well as verbal instruction—Chinese proverb

I will be speaking about effective communication in all sections of the G.A.M.E. chapters, but I'd like to address this topic of communication in light of the qualities of leadership. A good leader has to have a can-do attitude and be an effective listener and speaker. This is true in both Chinese and American cultures. In Chinese culture, it is more customary to be indirect and vague in your communication. And it is more acceptable in Chinese culture to say "perhaps" or "maybe" when a person really means "no." I much prefer the direct way of Americans. We Americans are clearer, more concise, and more transparent so that there is nobody left wondering what's going on. This is especially true for a leader. We can't stand on ceremony and leave people guessing.

Of course, we must practice *zhong yong* and follow the path of balance. We should attempt a soft approach, even in our directness. It is important to communicate delicately and foster graciousness and humility in our written and spoken communication so as not to offend.

But a hallmark of a great leader is being able not only to make uncomfortable decisions but also to engage in what Heifetz calls "courageous conversations."[29] It is difficult for most people to engage in conflict, speak to disruptive people, or say something that could be potentially hurtful, but we must! As Heifetz says, "We must engage above and below the neck. . . . Courage requires all of you: heart, mind, spirit, and guts."[30] We must be transparent, brave, and bold, and we must be able to be comfortable as well as uncomfortable.

A FEW WORDS ABOUT MENTORS AND COACHES

He who asks is a fool for five minutes, but he who does not ask remains a fool forever.—Chinese proverb

Frustration and confusion abound when you are starting a business and assuming a leadership role; a learning curve awaits you. You will fall down, you will question yourself, you will feel as if you've bit off more than you can chew; I call this "going through the pain patch." I've been there, and reached out to a business coach, but it seemed to take way too much time for me to explain my issues. I sometimes couldn't pinpoint what the problems were or didn't even know what questions to ask. And sometimes it didn't seem to be the right advice! I thought, "Man, I could have just used that time on the phone to figure it out myself." I now am a mentor to nurse entrepreneurs, and I know that consulting really must be an art form. I know how important it is to choose the right questions to ask and how critical it is to facilitate the most efficient and meaningful meetings with busy clients. Coaching is transforming.

I have been drawn to transforming all my life. I started transforming patients to move through their fears as a surgical nurse. Yet it was in my years serving the Guilin City Science and Technology Association when my focus on transforming first came into play. I helped local entrepreneurs transform their businesses by connecting with worldwide organizations. I even hosted a television program to reveal Chinese cultural and business opportunities, which was broadcast across China. Since then, I have found my true path of transformation! I have had quite a few people come to me and tell me how much their businesses have grown, and how much their quality of life has improved through their discussions with me. Some of them stated that this new way of thinking—the Monkey King's growth mind-set—awakened within them their deepest callings, which fundamentally changed their way of viewing the world around them and ultimately brought them success in business and personal life.

I define transformation as a fundamental shift from a fixed mind-set to a growth mind-set in your relationship with yourself, your business, and the world around you. It is a process that makes practical changes in order to cultivate your growth mind-set, promote your ability to learn from and even enjoy challenges, improve your business skills, and ultimately achieve your optimal quality of life while serving others. This growth mind-set takes your life and business to a different level of effectiveness, helps you achieve your personal and business goals, and improves you and the world around you. You are welcome to visit our website at NursingCareerConsultants.com.

Here is an example: One of my clients, a small-business owner who runs a medical supply business, was in crisis mode. Her once booming business seemed to be erupting in her face. She knew that she had excellent, unique products—and knew that the market was hot, which was confirmed with our research and assessment. However, she complained that people didn't like her, and she wondered what was wrong with her personality. She had always thought she was a likeable kind of gal and had always received very favorable feedback and positive interactions with customers and vendors at trade shows. She had no problem making contacts and making sales. But she said that employees would quit suddenly, sales reps and stores dropped her, and once she even overheard an intern call her an undesirable word.

However, after speaking with her, it became apparent that, while she was excellent at designing her unique products, promoting them, and teaching customers how to use them, she was completely disorganized. Her skills didn't lie in the business management and communication side of things. The problem wasn't her personality; the problem was that she was letting people down by missing deadlines, with her shoddy bookkeeping, and her disorganized projects. This left her sales reps and employees working overtime, wasting hours waiting, and communicating incorrect information to retailers and other key players. The good news is: through implementing the business-transforming plan we designed for her, she got herself to concentrate on her strengths and become the real boss she wanted to be quickly!

A conversation with a wise person is worth of ten years'
study of books.—Chinese proverb

If you are new to building a business, or your business seems stalled, there is no shame in contacting an expert who can mentor you through the process. In fact, it will save you a lot of time, headaches, and money if you do! Sometimes we just need a nudge in the right direction—or a bridge over troubled water. So you don't waste your time or money.

BE SURE OF THE FOLLOWING BEFORE YOU CONTACT A CONSULTANT:

1. Have your objectives for starting a business—or what your goals are for your existing business. Consultants need to generate insights on how things should be done, but their ideas must support your objectives.

2. Find out if the consultant or coach has real nursing business experience and is able to align this with your product, process, or service. Too many consultants out there think that they can help everyone by teaching theories and trying to fit everyone in a one-size-fits-all mold. The consultant must understand your unique story. Growing a nursing business is quite different than growing a general business.

3. Determine what the philosophy of the consultant is. You'd be surprised by how many consultants just bark out ideas without really listening, caring, and thinking about your long-term success. You want someone who is dedicated to your success and who truly cares about your success. My personal philosophy as a consultant is to be a business-management partner who is truly looking out for you every step of the way.

4. Be specific and detailed about your outcome and result—and get your goal down in writing! You need to be clear about what you will gain at the end of the training or coaching program.

5. Make sure the consultant is approachable and result-driven and that you can count on his or her respect for your hard work and investment.

I recommend that you consider our Nursing Business Success Systems to obtain an objective, expert viewpoint on your goals, mission, mind-set, business plan, and operations. Many entrepreneurs told me that a neutral, experienced expert can assess strengths and weakness that they, being in the middle of the fray, simply cannot. You can check out more information from our website: NursingCareerConsultants.com.

Now, let's get to the step no. 2 of the G.A.M.E.—assessing the field!

Chapter Nine

Game Plan Step No.2: Assessing the Field

WU, YOU, AND ALL YOU DO

....

Without study, you stand facing a wall and
your management of affairs will run into trouble.

—Chinese proverb

....

AS MONKEY KING KNEW, IT'S important to carefully assess the field before you start your game: What are the trends in your specialty? What is the best strategy for your particular product or service? What is the geographic, demographic, and psychographic target? How do you best reach your ideal patients or clients?

Finding the answers is an exciting process of researching, brainstorming, reading, drafting, and developing ideas. It's also a recursive process, meaning that one piece of research may change many aspects of the process. You may, for instance, decide to offer the same service in a different location because of market demand, and then this alters the marketing message. Some may find the process of discovery, change, focus, expansion, and rediscovery messy and daunting, but I find it exhilarating.

But before you have all the fun of creating your business plan, product or service, marketing strategies, operating strategies, and the like, take a moment to meditate, reflect, and write—again.

The most successful leaders think holistically—that is the *wu*; you position yourself solidly so that you can have great vision and can see everything without your ego getting in the way. Ask yourself what is unique about you, your product or service, your style, your knowledge, your experiences, and your story. If you want to stand out in every way with your business, if you want to attract your ideal clients, you must discern what makes your business unique. One way of doing this is to purposefully elicit feedback from everyone with whom you have contact.

Some people believe that their products or services are the same as everyone else's and that there is nothing new under the sun, but when you really dig deep and gather feedback to define and refine your stuff, you will see that you, my fellow nurse, have an incredible knowledge bank that you can leverage to achieve entrepreneurial success. We nurses truly forget how much we know! So, if your friends don't think of that, you should be sure to include that in your service statement.

I know that I may be this tough-minded, results-driven, goal-oriented, reflective, fearless person you ever met. I know that I enjoy a rather simple lifestyle; however, I love bright colors, beautiful art, and lively music. And I am a caring nurse entrepreneur who wants to help other nurse entrepreneurs. You will see my elements in every facet of Nursing Career Consultants. After you have done your homework and solidified your target market and product or service, ask what is unique about what you offer.

▶ Is it that your service is effective and efficient?
▶ Is it that the market you serve is unique?
▶ Is your product unique? Does it guarantee a result? Is it tailor made for certain people or made of a unique substance?
▶ Is the whole experience unique? Does it offer unique benefits and special touches?
▶ Are your price or payment options unique, with a low price, guaranteed add-ons, or premium price?

In this chapter, I have outlined many strategies for market research, but before you start taking action, remember to know thyself—and to thine own self be true.

HOT TUBS, SPEARS, AND SHIELDS

The shadow will never be so completely hidden that it is not seen
by someone.—Chinese proverb

Most of us nurse entrepreneurs will be doing some very sensitive work. Remember that we are caring for people, and the people we serve don't like to be alienated or disappointed. This goes not only for the product or service but also for the marketing message. I am reminded of an anecdote a friend told me about when she and her husband were younger, and they were struggling to make ends meet. They had two small children and a new mortgage and were still paying off student loan debt.

At one point, they decided to switch homeowner's insurance to save money, and they decided to call around to local agents for quotes. One agent's message on his answering machine said this: "Hi. You've reached Kent and Brenda! We'd love to help you with your insurance needs, but we are probably having fun in the hot tub, on the boat, or on the links! Please leave a message, and we'll get back with you as soon as we can pull ourselves away." My friend was stunned.

She thought: "I can't even afford new curtains, and this guy is bragging about his expensive stuff and hobbies? It doesn't sound like he has time for the people who are helping him pay for his Jacuzzi, speedboat, or tee times!" Now perhaps Kent and Brenda thought that the message was that they were fun, carefree, and affluent people. But what it sounded like instead was that they were insensitive to the needs of the potential customer. You should think closely about whether this is the type of unique message that would appeal to your target prospects. Word of mouth is the strongest marketing available. Clearly Kent and Brenda need to look inside themselves, plan deliberately, and find the right way.

Another big mistake that small-business owners make is marketing to everybody. If you believe your market is everybody, you will struggle to attract people who will actually use your services. When it comes to nurses, for instance, specialists usually receive more compensation than generalists. It's important to decide what area or areas you're going to serve and become the expert in that area.

Don't try to be all things to all people. Here is a famous Chinese story about this very topic:

SPEARS AND SHIELDS

Once a man was trying to sell spears and shields. He held high his shields first and boasted, "Look at the best shields! See the design! The quality! And the shape! No spear on earth can pierce them! The surest protection for your body! Buy one to be a respected warrior!"

Then he put down his shields and raised one of his spears and shouted, "This is the sharpest spear there is. It is a spear of death! Any shield, no matter how hard it might be, can be penetrated by this spear with a single blow!"

This sounded nice. But one onlooker stepped forward and asked, "Excuse me, but if I use your spear to strike your shield, what will then happen?"

The advertiser rolled his eyeballs, opened his mouth wide, and couldn't find any good answer. He withdrew instead.

You certainly cannot be all things to all people. Pick your niche and go with it. This little story goes back to deep insight, consistency, development of uniqueness, and starting at the end—and this story is also about integrity. If you try to provide something that doesn't have value or if you market it deceptively, believe me, your clients will know.

YOU KNOW WHO YOU ARE, BUT WHO ARE THEY?

It is said that if you know your enemies and know yourself, you will not be imperiled in a hundred battles; if you do not know your enemies but do know yourself, you will win one and lose one; if you do not know your enemies nor yourself, you will be imperiled in every single battle.—Sun Tzu, *The Art of War*

Don't be like the silly spear and shield salesman, and don't be like Brenda and Kent: identify a market, learn as much as you can about it, create a product or service and marketing message tailored to this market and its needs, and be consistent.

Step One: The first step is to learn about your potential market. Conduct a market analysis. You don't need to hire a fancy firm for this. You just need Google and a library. You can look at copious amounts of free demographics and trends data through the Small Business Development Center Network (www.sbdcnet.org). This should be your first stop.

For the health care market, you can research health trends through governmental agencies' websites, like those of the World Health Organization (www.who.org) or the Centers for Disease Control (www.cdc.gov), the Assistant Secretary for Planning and Evaluation (aspe.hhs.gov). I also would recommend, depending upon your field, that you look up what your state and local governmental agencies are concerned about. For instance, if your county health department is running copious amounts of health workshops for people with certain ailments, that is indicative of a trend—a new market—and you will want to think of how you can best help those potential clients!

You can also access recent academic journals and trade publications at your local library in order to determine the hottest trends. Look also at your specific field's websites, blogs, and newsletters for information.

Furthermore, you can consult the *Standard Rate and Data Service*—which is available at all libraries. This is a book that breaks down lists by state, demographics, and the number of people who have bought a product. Your librarian will be happy to help.

Step Two: The second step is to research your market saturation. Find out what other people in your field are up to. Notice that I suggested you research the market, trends, and data *first*, before your research your competitors. This is because you don't want to be just like them. You want to be one step ahead of them by noticing trends and gaps that they may be too busy or blind to see. Researching competitors is usually just a simple Google search that will yield excellent results; most of the time, the companies' forms, prices, locations, services, licenses, and overall business model are all right on their website. But you should also see what they are doing on social media, television, radio, specialty magazines, and direct mailers. Keep your ears and eyes open for what the buzz is!

Step Three: The third step is to learn about your ideal clients. Conduct extensive research to uncover the truth about the daily lives, opinions, and frustrations of your target audience. For instance, if you are considering being an independent case manager, you would want to survey the case managers, patients, and members of management teams to paint a picture of what your niche market wants and what messages might appeal to them. So, for instance, if you learn that complicated forms are daunting for elderly clients, you could say in your marketing message that you create ease in case management through a simplification of forms. Or if you learned that their top concern is that they want dependable in-home visits at certain, convenient times, that information could influence your service and message as well. You could advertise: "Convenient, consistent times that work for you!" It is easier to sell bread to a hungry man than to convince him that he is hungry.

Always look at a clear picture of your target market—don't go on assumptions or stereotypes. The more data and information the better. When you know exactly who you are selling to, you can address their values, cultural references, tastes, and mind-set. Furthermore, you can go back and refine your products and services again to make sure that they meet a clear need.

KEEP IT SIMPLE

Simplicity of character is the most natural result of profound thought.—Chinese proverb

After you have defined your core values, set your goals, created your product or service, culled trend data, determined your market, and then refined your goals, products, and services again, you will want to solidify your brand name. A brand is a visible, unifying thought that both you and others have when they think of your product or service. It is a promise to your consumer. So the name should be personalized, unique, and reflective of your brand.

The thing is, it's difficult for busy people to hold too much information in their heads about companies. We know that Coca-Cola sells soda, and it has consistent quality; we don't really need to know that it sells thousands of other products and services all over the world. All of the complexities behind the brand would be overwhelming to think about. We just need to keep it simple.

Your name and your brand should have a simple, unifying theme that people can easily identify with, associate positively with, and remember easily. Nancy Haberstich's idea for Nanobugs is an excellent example of this. The very name means fun, but it also cleverly refers to the science behind her services and products. The name for our training and coaching company is Nursing Career Consultants, which refers to simple, effective, and powerful ways to optimize career results. It is reflective of our helping nurse entrepreneurs to reclaim their respect, freedom, and prosperity.

There are six different types of company names:

1. **Abstract, but a real word or phrase,** like Apple, Virgin, or Kayak even though the companies don't have anything to do with apples, virgins, or kayaks.

2. **Abstract, but a made-up word or phrase,** like Google, Adidas, or Pixar—which are nonsense words inspired by ideas or people's names.

3. **Associative, but a real word or phrase,** like Sprint, Redbox, and Amazon. These names have associated attributes but don't necessarily describe the products or services.

4. **Associative, but a made-up word or phrase,** like Wanelo (which stands for want, need, love) and Reddit (read it). These names offer associated attributes but don't necessarily describe the products or services.

5. **Descriptive, but a real word or phrase,** like General Motors, Bank of America, or United Technologies—pretty straightforward stuff.

6. **Descriptive, but a made-up word or phrase,** like YouTube, Microsoft, and Duolingo—these effectively describe the product or service: *you* will be on the *"tube"* (television); Microsoft offers small-scale (rather than mainframe) software solutions.

So many brand names are portmanteaus! For instance, the names:

▸ Instagram (*instant* + *gram*—or message)
▸ Walmart (*Walden* name + *supermart*)
▸ Costco (*cost-saving* + *company*)
▸ Qualcomm (*quality* + *communications*)
▸ Verizon (the Latin word *veritas*, meaning truth + the word *horizon*)

My point with these examples is twofold. Think about how easy it is to recall a famous logo and the product or service associated with it. That's a brand; we know its promise. My second point is that it is important to create a simple and unique name for your business.

It certainly could be your last name; that is *very* effective. In fact, my husband's full name was used for the life plan elder law business—which is customary in law. But there may be some problems with naming it after yourself:

1. Your name might not actually signify the brand of your product or service well. I think of a dentist whose last name was Hurt— he actually changed his last name and used an entirely different name for his practice.
2. If you sell the company, the new owners may not appreciate having your name as their brand.
3. There may be others with the same or a similar name.
4. Your name might not be memorable. Sure, if you have a unique name like Disney, Kroger, Trump, or Macy, you might be okay.

Whatever you do, keep it simple and reflective of your core values and image.

Now that you have selected a name for your business, you should deliberate about what word it should be associated with. In *The 22 Immutable Laws of Marketing*, authors Al Ries and Jack Trout claim that you will want to "'burn' your way into the mind by narrowing the focus to a single word or concept."[1] For instance, Kleenex *is* tissues. One word. And if you can't own the word for a product or service, you could own a quality or attribute. For instance, Domino's Pizza owns what word? Delivers! They offer home delivery. Ries and Trout say that focusing on one word is "the ultimate marketing sacrifice," but it is worth it.

You need to go back to thinking about what is unique about your product or service to find the right word or words for your brand.

GETTING THE WORD OUT THERE

Once you have solidified your market and have created a focus, get the word out there with great intention. You don't want to waste your time and money with mass marketing when it is a niche market. Every one of the following ideas can be customized to hit your target audience:

▶ Ads in newsletters, trade journals, online magazines, specialty websites

▶ Articles in trade, scholarly, general interest, or traditional news publications, magazines, or websites

▶ Sponsorship of teams, events, special events, concerts, sporting contest, trade conferences

▶ Association directories

▶ Freebies with your logo and contact information

▶ Personal appearances at gatherings and word of mouth

▶ YouTube videos

▶ Google AdWords

▶ News for doing something awesome

▶ Radio ads or call-in talk shows on AM, FM, satellite, or internet apps

▶ Television ads or appearances and interviews

▶ Referrals and testimonials from patients or clients

▶ Podcasts

▶ Participation in festivals, parades, and 5Ks with booths, floats, or freebies

▶ Pro bono work

▶ Banner ads or pop-up ads on blogs or trade websites

▶ LinkedIn ads or professional blogs or interest groups

▶ Social media: Pinterest, Facebook, Twitter, Instagram, or MySpace

▶ Yellow Pages or free White Pages

▶ Wraps or ads on sides of cars

▶ Webinars

▶ Emails

▶ Trade or conference exhibition vendor, keynote speaker, workshop presenter, or sponsor

- Public expo vendor or sponsor
- Donations to nonprofits
- Flyers distributed to homes or businesses or posted in public spaces
- Yahoo! stores
- Stickers, bumper stickers, T-shirts, or bracelets
- Special events
- FedEx envelopes or special gifts
- Infomercials
- Television shows like *All-American Makers* or *Shark Tank*
- Craigslist
- Billboards and signs
- Telemarketing
- Amazon.com
- Flyer inserts in newspapers, magazines, coupon mailers, or mail-order shipments
- Blogging
- Catalog spots
- Press releases

CHASING THE SUN

Great things are not done by impulse, but by a series of small things brought together.—Chinese proverb

I believe that an intact marketing and operating system is the key to success and leads to peace of mind. What I mean by intact is not random and impulsive but incredibly consistent and dependable. An intact marketing and operating system allows you to predict the stability and the steady flow of your business income, which ultimately leads you to the optimal level of success. Consistency and dependability are my birthright. It all started when I was a little girl, sitting with my wise business genius yie yie (grandfather). He used to tell me an ancient story about acting impulsively.

GIANT KUAFU CHASES THE SUN

Long ago, soon after time began, there was a brave and giant man named Kuafu whose strength knew no bounds. Every day the sun would rise in the east and travel across the sky and then disappear beyond the western horizon. But Kuafu wondered, where does it come from and where does it hide itself? When darkness fell, Kuafu would become sad. One night he thought, "I do not like nighttime. All life falls into a slumber. If I could catch the sun, then I could keep night as bright as day! The plants could grow forever, and it would always be warm. I would never have to sleep again."

The very next day, Kuafu awoke as soon as the sun arose in the east. He ran as fast as his strong legs could take him toward the sun. Over several thousand miles he raced and raced without rest. Finally, he chased the sun to the Yu Valley where it set every day, but Kuafu was very thirsty from his exhaustion. His thirst grew and soon it became overwhelming. He had never known a thirst so strong, and his body seemed to dry up to nothing. Kuafu found the nearest stream and drank it dry, but it was not enough.

With a giant's stride, he quickly reached the mighty Huanghe River. He drank it dry, but again, it was not enough. He continued toward the Great Sea—surely it held water enough to quench his thirst. On his journey, he drank dry every well and every stream and every lake he came across, but finally his thirst overpowered him, and Kuafu fell to the ground.

In a fit of anger he made a swing at the sun with a branch of a peach tree. Before the branch reached the sun, Kuafu died of thirst. The sun set in the Yu Valley as usual, and night fell over Yu Valley. When the sun rose again, Kuafu's body had been transformed into a mountain range. The peach tree branch extended from his side and formed a peach tree grove.

To this day, the peaches in this grove are sweet and moist, always ready to relieve the thirst of those who would chase the sun.

I really like Kuafu because he thinks big! There is no crime in that. In fact, as I started the skin care, cosmetic surgery, and women's health business in China, I was truly thinking big. In the early 1990s there were only a few people who even knew what plastic surgery was! Creating awareness of this unique market and reaching my desired prospects was a big challenge. However, I kept my *yei yei's* wisdom in mind instead of chasing the sun.

First, I came up with the idea of promoting the skin care and the cosmetic surgery service together as one focused business, with the niche idea of creating specialty acne treatment products and services. I interviewed a few local hospitals' pharmacies (all pharmacies were run by hospitals at that time in China) so that we could develop our own unique brand of anti-acne products.

With our advertisements about skin care and our high standards of operating room aseptic techniques, we attracted innumerable acne patients. We hit almost 100 percent in patient satisfaction in treating acne! And what is more exciting is that at least 90 percent of those clients signed up for their annual skin care maintenance service with us and nearly 50 percent of them attended our cosmetic surgery educational workshops. Because we had a consistent product, consistent results, and a steady business income stream, I was able to develop a higher level of marketing and operating system.

I was tempted at times to throw more products and services into the mix, but I realized that I should slow down, not chase the sun, and build a solid foundation for what we were doing well. We were able to branch out our services, but not before we had a stable foundation for a period of time. It's interesting that a stable, consistent product and service for our clients created stability and consistency for the business, which then gave me personal stability. What I put out, I got back!

Sometimes consistency can feel like boredom for some small-business owners. There once was a client who was running an extremely successful ad campaign. After about six months, he wanted to develop an entirely new campaign. When asked why, he simply said, "I'm bored with the one we have."

What? Losing money is a good reason to start a new campaign. Boredom is not.

Avoid this mistake by remembering that what is old to you is new to an untapped target market. If you have a promotion that is consistently getting you results, stick with it until results show you it's time for change, and test new promotions before you abandon the current one. Then track results. Never swap a current promotion—or a product or service—with a new one that hasn't been tested.

LILY'S TIPS FOR EFFICIENT, EFFECTIVE MARKETING

Aside from my insistence on being authentic, creative, and consistent and beginning at the end, here are some other tips I've gleaned:

▸ A client who finds you is more likely to actually employ you or use your products than one you find.

▸ Generate leads by providing positive information about solutions to existing problems.

▸ People who have purchased from you before are your great referral sources for new clients; keep excellent records.

▸ Warm leads are better than cold calls.

TIME IS OF THE ESSENCE

Man who waits for roast duck to fly into mouth must wait very, very long time.—Chinese proverb.

Since I was a child, I have played the cello. It is such a beautiful, elegant instrument. There is something so magical about setting the metronome. It is like a heartbeat measuring out the tenuous moments until I bring bow to string. And as I enter the musical piece, I know that in music, timing is everything.

Marketing is about timing too. Oftentimes we prepare and prepare for the right time to begin, and we listen and listen, and wait and wait almost hypnotically to begin. If you are too concerned with getting all the details right (testing, focus groups, and market surveys) you'll lose your opportunities.

It is like that checkerboard I mentioned earlier. If you hesitate before moving, or neglect to move promptly, your men will be wiped off the board by time. Many believe that you succeed by being the best, but this is a fallacy. You are more likely to succeed by being there first. Let me assure you that there has never been a better time for our nurse entrepreneurs to create the most desired market we dreamed of.

HOW TO GET YOUR IDEA TO MARKET

You might have a brilliant idea like Dan Tribastone but wonder: how do I get this made? Look in your area for maker spaces, job shops, maker fairs, or entrepreneurship labs where you will be able to make a prototype or connect with someone who can. Amy Hickman started asking around among friends, neighbors, and family members. You would be surprised by who might come out of the woodwork. You could also contact your local community college or university. Many have tech shops and engineering labs. Additionally, 3-D printers are everywhere these days (even in community libraries) and many engineering students or professionals can assist you in developing a prototype. Be wary of online invention assistance outfits. They may be legitimate, but others may not be. Ask for references before you enter any contract.

It is best to register your patent with the US Patent and Trademark Office before you get deep into the process—then you can find out if it has already been invented. (Or you could always go on my favorite television show: *Shark Tank*!) Attorneys are a requirement for patents and copyrights. According to Dr. Anne York, director of the Bioscience Entrepreneurship Program at Creighton University College of Business Administration, this is an essential part of the process. "Patenting, trademarking, or copyrighting ideas can be very important, especially for inventions that are costly to develop. If you want to sell or license your invention to someone else, then you need to have protected it. Laws vary from country to country, but in the U.S., as soon as an idea is publicly disclosed, you only have one year to protect it by filing a patent. You need to protect your invention so that someone else can't come along and patent it and use it in ways that you might not want them to. If you patent an item, you have control over how it is used."[2]

If you have an idea for a smartphone app, there are many app ideas for nurses (such as the Uber-type nursing apps) that aren't just apps. They are visiting-nurse services that happen to use an app. But many apps are still waiting to be created! These websites might be very helpful to you:

▸ App Inventor, www.appinventor.mit.edu or www.appinventor.org

▸ Entrepreneurship Lab, New York City, http://elabnyc.com

▸ Partners Healthcare: Innovations, http://innovation.partners.org

THE SEVEN STAR PARK

The beginning of wisdom is to call things by their right names.—Chinese proverb

Located at the foot of the Putuo Hill in my scenic hometown of Guilin is the beautiful Seven Star Park—a popular and beautiful attraction built in the fifth century. It got its name from the seven peaks that are said to resemble the star pattern of the Big Dipper.

The park is endowed with elegant mountains, clear water, a miraculous stone forest, deep and serene valleys, plentiful animals, plants, and valued cultural relics. Everywhere you look is an appealing special feature. The Flower Bridge (*Hua Qiao*)— which every summer is showered with real blooms—is the main entrance to the park. It is an elegant arched structure dating from the Song Dynasty (960–1279) that crosses the confluence of East River and Li River Stream that passes through the park.

The park features calligraphy carvings within the hills' caves—which are said to be the work of important calligraphers from the Tang (AD 618–907), Ming (AD 1368–1644) and Qing (AD 1644–1911) dynasties.

Putuo Mountain, where Avalokitesvara Bodhisattva is worshiped, is the main body of the park. It abounds with caves and pavilions. From every vista high and low is a breathtaking scene to behold. This park, which has been popular for over a thousand years, attracts tourists from all over the world and is considered the crown jewel of the province.

One day, when I was talking to some hotel managers, I told them of this famous and beautiful Seven Star Park in my beloved hometown. They laughed and said, "We've heard of five-star accommodations, but what is seven-star?" You know, I had never thought of it like that until then, but really, the Seven Star Park really is a seven-star park. The name fits it so well because it is beyond any park I have ever seen or heard of. This is no ordinary park: it has been a popular place for millions of people for over a thousand years. They may have laughed and been confused and incredulous, but now I say "Why not?" When creating a small business, we must surpass what is expected (merely five stars), and create a brand that is far beyond what others are doing! We must create products and services that are like Seven Star Park: that have amazing, unique features that work together harmoniously and that many people clamor to use—so much so that marketing really isn't necessary.

Chapter Ten

Game Plan Step No.3: Monitoring it All

STRATEGY AND TACTICS

....

Strategy without tactics is the slowest route to victory.
Tactics without strategy is the noise before defeat.

—Sun Tzu, The Art of War

....

WHEN YOU MOVE FROM BEING an individual entrepreneur to managing larger operations and overseeing the work of others, you face new challenges. The truth is that the skills that made you a great independent nurse won't necessarily make you a great business manager. As a business owner, up to 40 percent of your time may be spent doing administrative work. You are not only being the leader and visionary, but also running the day-to-day business: keeping financial records, booking patients or clients, selling products or services—and if you have employees, hiring, training, supervising, and communicating with them. Building the life plan elder law practice brick by brick and growing to a multimillion-dollar company in just a few years meant that we needed clear procedural systems for workflow, communication, boundaries, and roles—as well as policies for keeping everything moving smoothly.

We nurses are accustomed to fixing problems, saving people, and diffusing critical situations. That being said, we are very good at observing, recording, communicating, setting boundaries, and multitasking. We can become excellent managers! There will always be pain patches in every level of growth, but with proactive strategies, you will be able to monitor it all efficiently, fairly, and with grace.

ELEPHANTS AND STONES

Pick up a stone, only to drop it on one's toes. But treat others well, and they will help hold the stone for you.—Chinese proverb

At its core, leadership is an exercise in creating a sustainable culture or changing a culture if necessary. It's about bridging gaps: gaps between you and your team, gaps between behaviors and desired outcomes, and gaps between reality and aspiration. Thus you should understand clearly the culture you wish to create by going back to your *wu*—your values, mission, and vision. You must know and establish your culture before you can create effective processes and policies for actually managing your team. Because if you create an inviting, inspiring, supportive, and inclusive culture, you will get the best results from whatever systems you put in place. Here is a story of this very concept.

THE STORY OF ELEPHANT TRUNK HILL

There is a story told in my hometown of Guilin. It is said that the very hill I used to run up for volleyball training, Elephant Trunk Hill, is the embodiment of a god elephant, who was once ridden by the Emperor of Heaven. It was separated from the emperor during a battle and was stranded in Guilin with severe wounds. A local couple saved its life and nursed it back to health. But after it experienced such hospitality, and after it drank from the sweet water of the Li River, the elephant fell in love with the life there and decided not to return to the heavenly palace. The emperor bestowed a pagoda to help it suppress evils and protect people. It still has never left Guilin and to this day its home is known as Elephant Trunk Hill.

When you create an inviting, warm, open, and consistent work environment, management decisions will have greater reception and procedures will be followed for the greater good—because you are working together in harmony.

Think about the saying, "Pick up a stone, only to drop it on one's toes. But treat others well, and they will help hold the stone for you." For a manager, this means that if you create a positive environment and a fair system, the weight of the business will be shared by the team.

These days, an informal atmosphere is a competitive advantage for attracting talent and increasing productivity. People tend to flourish with less rigid and more natural processes and spaces. This doesn't mean one should totally abandon the usual framework of agendas, reports, and policies; it means one should allow for spontaneous communication and for joy in the environment. Remember this when you create your organizational structure.

CHANNELS

Flowing water never goes bad; door hubs never gather
termites.—Chinese proverb

A successful organization must have an effective and sustainable operational strategy that stems from strategic planning and organizational vision—and that meshes with the established culture. Workflow, boundaries, channels of communication, and roles within the organization should be methodically planned. Think of it this way: Let's say that you have a small office of five employees. They all have their own positions and responsibilities, and when you are there, you can delegate tasks and supervise their work so that all is well. But what if you are gone or tied up—who makes decisions then? What happens if a client calls and you can't provide client service—and no one else is trained to do so? What is the flow of communication when all have very different— or very similar—roles? What if there is no accountability for achieving outcomes or meeting deadlines? This can lead to low morale: when some are making decisions that others should be making, or when some are making off-base decisions, and when some are working harder than others. The list of problems goes on.

I liken my operational strategy design to the artificial canals of China—especially the Ling Canal. Located forty-one miles to the northeast of my hometown of Guilin, it is one of the world's most ancient integrated canals. It was built under the patronage of the great emperor Qin Shi Huang—who also built the Great Wall of China, and it was considered, at the time, to be an equally monumental accomplishment. The canal was constructed with the aim of connecting the Li and Xiang Rivers in order to facilitate the trade and commerce of Qin Shi Huang's empire. The canal is an example of the advanced architectural and engineering ideas and skills that ancient Chinese society possessed some 2,000 years ago. The two largest rivers of China, the Yangtze and the Pearl, flow into the canal.

Because of the difference in the levels of water streaming from the two different river systems, the engineers created the first known system of locks to transport barges and boats to the other systems. The technological feat of hand-digging canals, ports, and locks increased so much more than trade in the region. Innovative ideas, culture, language, stories, and so much more was transmitted along these channels. These exchanges of information likely would have happened somewhere along the line, but not with the speed and ease that the canals afforded. This is why structuring operations with great intent is important, not just for fostering innovations, forging relationships, increasing trade, and sharing missions, but also to increase the speed at which it can all be achieved!

Just like the canal, there are now huge advancements in how things get done. Hundreds of organizations all around the world are now being run in a radically different way—a way that is more responsive to clients' needs. It is a way that is more fun for people doing the work, and that makes more money than running a company in the traditional way. This new system differs from traditional top-down models of governance.

HOW TO CREATE A RADICAL NEW CHANNEL SYSTEM

1. Empower self-organizing teams that report to other teams as well as to leadership.

2. All members up and down are held responsible for outcomes; their number one goal is client, or patient satisfaction.

3. All teams share excitement, ideas, observations, and solutions; lateral sharing, rather than hierarchical sharing, builds relationships, innovation, and a sense of purpose.

4. Teams and leaders perform their own assessments, create their own goals, and hold themselves accountable (see chapter 11 for more on accountability).

5. Collectively, the teams create a logical, easy system with policies—keeping in mind vision, culture, and the idea of starting at the end. These are then shared with others, for transparency and avoiding siloing of information are top priorities of a radical management system.

6. The management ensures transparency, efficiency, communication, self-improvement, and accountability—as well as modeling the mission and values—at every level. This is done with continuous conversations, questions, and stories.[1]

FLOW

In order for the channels of productivity and communication to flow with ease, there are several things a manager or leader must do to lay a solid interlocking and self-reinforcing foundation:

1. **Build the teams strategically, operationally, and organizationally.** Start with an overarching strategy in which each team member has a sharply defined, intensely shared, and purposeful understanding of what they are supposed to do and how this works with the larger aspirations of the team and the organization.

2. **Create a sense of ownership** and buy-in by all members of the team. We all have the same goal, and we should all know that we matter in the outcomes and our voices will be heard. Leaders, managers, and team leaders should make a point of communicating and listening at all times, and they should inspire, lead, and encourage autonomy. More on this in the next chapter.

3. **Implement process observation of the existing systems** using self-evaluations, data, and observation of meetings. Being the process observer of a team meeting, for instance, is an important role, as it ensures that the agenda was followed, all voices were heard, the topics stayed on track, the decisions were based on consensus and were recorded, the vision and mission were adhered to, action items were delegated, and time was valued. Anyone can perform this role—except the person calling the meeting and the recorder who is taking the minutes and making note of action items. The manager's role is to model the process and ensure that the process is valued.

4. **Drive operational accountability.** The real test of a high-performing team's capacity lies in the formal and informal practices that are at work across team members, particularly around clarifying decisions and flows of communication and information. It is important to observe, but also to map and track what is getting done by when by whom. It's all about credibility and confidence. (See chapter 11 for more on this.)

5. **Maintain a commitment to long-range planning.** All team leaders should schedule important meetings, create policies and procedures, and make long-term goals as far as twelve months out. Periodical reminders of vision, mission, and goals are important. The manager's role is to oversee consistency and long-range actions.

6. **Establish clear roles and responsibilities.** This is a tricky one when working in teams. We don't want to pigeonhole employees, and we want to encourage pairs, triads, and larger groups working together for common goals. When we all have defined roles and responsibilities, there is little doubt where the boundaries for accountability lie. The duty of the manager and leader is to define, remind, encourage, challenge, and hold accountable—but not in a hammer-coming-down way. Managers and employees should have a sense of partnership and shared vision for organizational excellence and collective goals.

7. **Establish a healthy regard for energy management.** Organizations are demanding more and more from their team members, and employees are trying to comply, but the usual methods—longer hours, weekends, forgoing vacations—don't work. Employees become exhausted and sick and tune out. Then they leave for other jobs. The following rituals were designed by researchers Tony Schwartz and Catherine McCarthy to replenish employees' energy—and lead to greater productivity and profits: taking brief breaks at specific intervals; expressing appreciation to others (which fills up the bucket of goodwill); reducing interruptions (turning off email, Internet, and phone for an announced period of time);[2] allowing time for rest and recuperation;[3] and spending time on activities people do best and enjoy most.[4] The manager's role here is to model energy management, express gratitude for accomplishments, codify—or at least encourage—energy management techniques, and respect the breaks of others.

8. **Emphasize smart time management.** One of the manager's main roles is to ensure that there isn't redundancy in work activities and communications and that work is being prioritized logically, in accordance with the mission and goals. Since the manager isn't creating the ideas, there is a sense of objectivity that may not exist within a team. By pointing out lack of efficiency or improper sequencing of duties, the manager can help to avoid wasted time and energy.

9. **Encourage time for out-of-the-box thinking.** We can get so wrapped up in results, efficiency, and time management that we forget that our best ideas come from relaxation and being open. Build into every team a respect for true brainstorming, a place where there is no wrong answer. Encourage them to turn their editors off for great periods of time.

10. **Sustain momentum and deliver results.** Remember that aligning your people, plans, and practices around a shared purpose is not a one-time event but something that will require constant, ongoing management and improvement to sustain momentum and deliver results. See the "Assessment" section below for more on this.

MILLENNIALS REQUIRE LEADERS, NOT MANAGERS—WITHIN REASON

The largest group of employees is millennials. Born after 1980 and before 2000, these are the children of baby boomers, and they don't want to be managed, they want to be led—fearlessly, idealistically, and collaboratively.

The millennials' parents doted on them, heaped them with praise, and built up their sense of self-worth. Their childhoods were ultrasafe—with car seats, bike helmets, safety caps, and stranger danger. Their lives were filled with structured activities and meaningful dialogues. And they were weaned on video games, instant messaging, and Internet everything.

With Internet and smartphone technology, copious amounts of data and information are at their fingertips, but they tend to see this as random, a flood of information that they find difficult to navigate. Their curiosity and willingness to search for answers is a positive, but they need guidance on how to apply real-world skills to their everyday jobs.

For most millennials, work must have meaning. They may or may not commit to your organization, but they will commit to a higher purpose, a good cause, or a way to fulfill their calling.

About.com's Susan Heathfield noted that millennials "have a wonderful 'can-do' attitude, and positive personal self-image."[5] Be sure to encourage them, praise their efforts, and be accessible to them in ways that you may not have been for other employees. The boundaries are quite different with this group. For millennials, the line between work and personal time is one such boundary. One up-and-coming craft brewer said, "I work for them in everything I do because it is what I love—it is part of who I am. When I go to festivals, parties, or contests, I am researching, networking, and promoting their brand. I will answer emails and conduct research on my own time." Monitoring their every move and fretting about texting and Facebook time may be misplaced energy. For them, work life and personal life are one. This should be, of course, within reason. If you find productivity slipping off, adjustments should be made, but you might be surprised by the 2014 study that shows that using social media at work actually boosts productivity![6]

Millennials may grate on some people's nerves because of their lack of formality and their uncanny ability to look at systems in terms of webs instead of tiers (a fundamental baby boomer and Gen X trait), but they do deserve our respect. David Berg, COO of Carlson, set up a mentorship program where his millennial employees mentor him in order to make sense of future guests.[7]

Millennials grew up with their parents as their best friends and confidants. They don't see age or hierarchy the way previous generations do. It may feel uncomfortable to blur the lines of work life and personal life, but connecting with millennials on other levels and on different platforms will help to create a solid team. When you must set a boundary regarding access or communication, they respond with understanding to the need for time with family, prior commitments, or unplugging and going off the grid. They very much understand those priorities.

If you give millennials respect and responsibility, they will live up to your expectations. Give them information and tools to succeed. They want to know what's going on, how they can help, and how their jobs fit into the organization's purpose, which ideally has a component that makes the world a better place.

Oftentimes millennials know that they want to be leaders; they know that they want to create a sustainable, kind world; they know that they want to use all of their talents, but they don't know how to get there. Try not to manage them so much as inspire, connect, and lead them. Try to draw them in rather than push them out—and you will be surprised by where they will take you!

ALL ABOARD

When planning for a year, plant corn. When planning for a decade, plant trees.
When planning for life, train and educate people.—Guan Zhong

In the next chapter, I will say more about training as a means of team building, but because training is so important for leaders and managers, I will address it here, too. There is no better time to impart your vision, your brand, your goals, and your expectations for excellence than when training prospective employees. As the organization grows bigger, team leaders will take over this role, but never let go of overseeing this aspect of your business, as it is the axis on which your business turns.

Your employees are the essential heartbeat of your business and should be treated as such. Approach training sessions as a divine opportunity to get to know their talent, model the culture, and share the dream.

THINK SMALL

A small hole not mended in time will become a big hole much more
difficult to mend.—Chinese proverb

Everyone talks about thinking big. I say to think small when it comes to monitoring it all. Ninety-nine percent of activities can be correctly done, but when 1 percent drops, your reputation is on the line, so it is imperative that the team members have planned everything starting from the end and are held accountable. I think of the systems that can truly trip you up and the solutions of creating different layers of communication (which is different than redundancy in work—which you want to avoid at all costs) and double-checking all systems, services, and products from the perspective of the client, patient, customer, or vendor.

Think of your business as the popular Jenga wooden block game. When you play this game, which requires you to remove blocks from a tall tower, you notice the small gaps and cracks in the foundation, because one little pull may not topple your building, but another one will. Be mindful of the weaknesses in your foundation. You must think small. I don't mean you should micromanage, but be alert to the functions, feedback, and data. Even with one or two employees, it is important to keep in mind the aforementioned attributes of flow. Well before there is a problem, put the policies and procedures in place and train everyone on them. Create a clear operational strategy and mind-set as if you were running a large corporation—and soon you will be!

It is very important to know how everything is supposed to flow, and you can give perspective on dynamics and remind them of the larger vision. That being said, it is important to know when to meddle and when to let go.

ASSESSMENT

We should never forget to take time to evaluate our business and take stock of where we are. There are many forms of assessment of the overall health of the company, but the old standby of SWOT still works quite well. SWOT stands for strengths, weaknesses, opportunities and threats, and it is an analytical framework that can help your new company face its greatest challenges and find its most promising markets. A SWOT analysis conducted by each team, or by leadership, or both focuses on the four elements included in the acronym, allowing companies to identify the forces that influence strategies, actions, or initiatives. Becoming aware of these positive and negative elements can aid companies in communicating what parts of a plan need to be recognized and prioritized.

When drafting a SWOT analysis, individuals typically create a table divided into four columns listing each impacting element side by side for comparison. Strengths and weaknesses won't typically match the opportunities and threats, though they tend to correlate somewhat, since they're tied together in some way. Pairing external threats with internal weaknesses can highlight the most serious issues faced by a company or team. Once you've identified your risks, the team leaders or management team can then decide whether it is most appropriate to eliminate the internal weakness by assigning company resources to fix the problems or to reduce the external threat by abandoning the threatened area of business and meeting it later after strengthening your business.[8]

SWOT LAYOUT

STRENGTHS			WEAKNESS

S   W

O   T

OPPORTUNITIES			THREATS

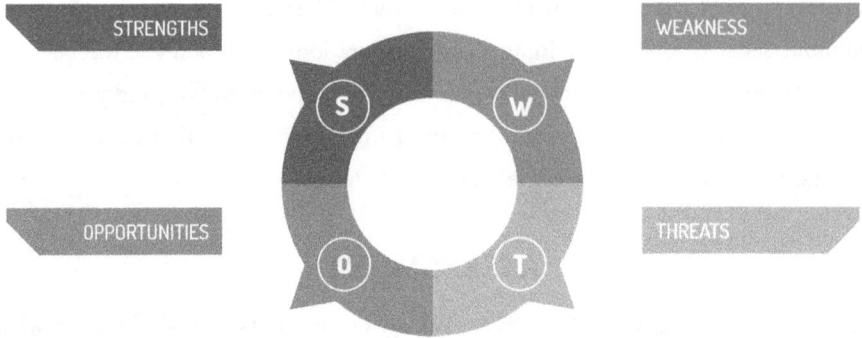

INTERNAL FACTORS

The first two letters in the acronym, S (strengths) and W (weaknesses), refer to internal factors, which means the resources and experience readily available to you. Examples of areas typically considered include:

- Financial resources, such as funding, sources of income, and investment opportunities
- Physical resources, such as your company's location, facilities, and equipment
- Human resources, such as employees, volunteers, and target audiences
- Access to natural resources, trademarks, patents, and copyrights
- Current processes, such as employee programs, department hierarchies, and software systems

I recommended fully analyzing your strengths and weaknesses first. Then the external factors can also be objectively assessed.

EXTERNAL FACTORS

External forces influence and affect every company, organization, and individual. Whether or not these factors are connected directly or indirectly to an opportunity or threat, it is important to take note of and document each one. External factors typically refer to things you or your company do not control, such as:

- Market trends, like new products and technology or shifts in audience need.
- Economic trends, such as local, national, and international financial trends
- Funding, such as donations, legislature, and other sources
- Demographics, such as a target audience's age, race, gender, and culture
- Relationships with suppliers and partners
- Political, environmental, and economic regulations

Once you fill out your SWOT analysis, you will need to come up with some recommendations and strategies based on the results. These strategies should be focused on leveraging strengths and opportunities to overcome weaknesses and threats. This is the area of strategy development where organizations have an opportunity to be most creative and where innovative ideas can emerge, but only if the analysis has been appropriately prepared.[9]

PLAN FOR THE FUTURE

It does not matter how slowly you go as long as you do not stop.—Confucius

Sometimes we get so caught up in day-to-day life, we forget that what we are doing is laying a foundation that reaches beyond this moment, this month, this year, or even this lifetime. We are creating legacies—not only of our enterprise, but also of the countless lives we have touched. When you think about all it takes to maintain a healthy business and life, you are reminded of the fact that you are building something that will impact generations; do not lose your resolve!

Chapter Eleven

Game Plan Step No.4: Empowering the Most Engaged Players

ASSEMBLE THE TEAM

Behind an able person there are always other able people.

—Chinese proverb

NOW YOU ARE THE EXPERT in your field, leader in your organization, marketing genius, and manager of processes; you may start out alone, but you won't grow without a talented and passionate team around you.

Make your organization stronger by acquiring, developing, encouraging, planning, and transitioning the talent of your team.

1. **Acquire.** Recruit, attract, and hire the right people.
2. **Develop.** Assess, train, and build skills and knowledge.
3. **Encourage.** Direct, support, recognize, and reward.
4. **Plan.** Monitor, assess, and plan career moves over time.
5. **Transition.** Migrate people to different roles as appropriate.

Rather than a top-down dictatorship, which brings in less revenue and retains fewer employees, a radical system of dynamic teamwork, fulfillment of passions, transparency, and shared vision helps a venture flourish. But you know, these new and radical methods are actually the same as Monkey King's. After he was released from the Five Finger Mountain he was no longer an arrogant and silly ruler; he became a member of a team consisting of a pig, a horse, a tortoise, and the monk. The five of them equally shared responsibilities and used their individual gifts to achieve their goal, bringing back the wisdom. When all are engaged, challenged, and respected, your enterprise will flourish—and everyone will flourish. But who do you trust to be on your team?

HIRE SOMEONE WHO BELIEVES IN YOUR VISION

What I learned especially over my eight years running the life plan elder law practice is that putting the right people into the right positions is actually even more important than developing a corporate or organizational strategy.

WHEN I HIRE, I USE THE FOLLOWING CRITERIA:

1. **Attitude.** Does the candidate possess a positive, willing, open, can-do mind-set?
2. **Self-Awareness or *wu*.** Does the person seem to know him- or herself and his or her existing strengths and areas for improvement?
3. **Aptitude.** Does the candidate have a natural ability for the position, or is there evidence that these abilities can be developed?
4. **Soft skills.** Did the interview show qualities of professionalism, timeliness, attention to detail, preparedness, politeness, and communication skills?
5. **Talent.** It is optimal for the candidate to possess skills and knowledge, but with the aforementioned traits, skills and knowledge can always be developed.

Number 5, talent, is what trips people up. We become so impressed with a candidate's résumé—their degrees, grades, achievements, and awards—that we become blinded to the fact that we can teach the trade, but we can't teach personality. Tesla founder Elon Musk told *Business Insider* that his biggest mistake when starting his first tech company was "Weighing too much on someone's talent and not someone's personality," Musk said. "I think it matters whether someone has a good heart."[1] When he says "heart," I think Musk is talking about all of those qualities that make for a great teammate: compassion, humility, perspective, drive, humor, and integrity.

Another thing we can't teach is a willingness to care about the company. It is hard to gauge whether there is buy-in to your vision and mission during a hiring process, but it is essential to try. As Jesse Jacobs, the founder of a chain of tea shops, states, "One thing I've learned over twelve years running Samovar Tea Lounge is the importance of having the right people on your team. It's worth the extra effort to find the right investors, employees, and vendors who believe in your company's mission and passionately desire to contribute to it—not just those who want to punch the clock or get their share of profits."[2]

Former Google employee and tech entrepreneur Gemma Young agrees. "Finding the right team is so, so crucial as an early-stage startup. We're finding that you can't just buy the best in the market. We are in the position of finding people with the shared vision and aren't necessarily looking for the large pay packet, that's the number one thing. I'd sacrifice skill set for the attitude, but luckily we haven't had to."[3]

But how do you do this? How can you possibly determine whether someone has the right attitude, shared vision, and passionately desires what you do?

Certainly we can glean a lot from a person's résumé—because it shows where they have placed their energy and time. And we all know the standard interview questions: "What are your strengths and weaknesses?" "Where do you see yourself in five years?" "What makes you right for this position?" Here are some more questions that get to the heart of the matter:

▸ What inspires you?
▸ This is our vision and mission. How would you help us fulfill that?
▸ We are passionate about creating supportive interactions with clients and their families. How would you execute this in your role?
▸ This is our vision and mission. What is your life vision and mission?
▸ If you had a million dollars, what would you do with it?
▸ If you had one word that describes you that we will write on the top of your candidate packet, what would it be and why?
▸ What brings you the most joy to your life?

These questions might tease out whether the candidate has a deep sense of *wu* and purpose—and whether these align with your vision and mission. You can also gauge the other elements of their EQ, such as social skills and empathy. In the end, when selecting the right candidate, I always rely on my *zhijue*, my sixth sense.

THE EIGHTEEN ARHATS

*It is hard to be even-minded and simple-hearted in all one's dealings
with others.—The Buddha*

There are so many aspects to one's personality: conflict-resolution style, communication style, personal motivations and values, interests and hobbies, leadership style, and work style and methods. Many people in a position of hiring someone are either unconsciously or consciously looking for certain personalities that will mesh with theirs. We can get tripped up hiring someone because of impressive credentials, and we can also get caught up in a pleasant—or similar personality. This is only natural, but I believe that to find the successful candidate, we must think of the following eighteen arhats.

Legend has it that the eighteen arhats were the original disciples of the Buddha who followed the eightfold path and attained enlightenment. These are important models of the Buddhist way and are depicted beautifully in Chinese art. Each has very unique attributes and personalities:

1. *Pindola the Bharadvaja* is depicted as dignified, thoughtful, composed, and content. He is above worldly pursuits.

2. *Kanaka the Vasta* is shown to be happy because he has cleared the universe of demons. His hands are raised in jubilation, and he is wild with joy.

3. *Kanaka the Bharadvaja* is depicted in majestic grandeur as joy descends from heaven. He is raising his bowl to receive happiness while glowing with joy and exultation.

4. *Nandimitra* is depicted as containing all of the miraculous power of the Buddha. He is forceful without being angry.

5. *Nakula* is shown quietly cultivating the mind. His face is calm and composed. He is serene and dignified.

6. *Bodhidharma* is one who travels the world fearlessly spreading the word of Buddha. He is concerned with saving humanity.

7. *Kalika* has a dignified air and a heart for humanity. He is ever-vigilant in trying to help the entire world.

8. *Vijraputra* is playful and free of inhibitions. He easily alternates between tension and relaxation. He rejoices in all living things.

9. *Gobaka* is shown with an open heart where Buddha lives. Each entity displays its power, but the two are not competing because Buddha's power is boundless.

10. *Pantha the Elder* is easy, comfortable, and completely content. He is shown yawning and stretching and in a state of omniscience.

11. *Rahula* is shown pondering and meditating. He understands it all. He is full of compassion and is free from worldliness and conventional thinking and behaving.

12. *Nagasena* is leisurely and contented, full of wit and humor and full of happiness, knowledge, and curiosity.

13. *Angida* is the Buddha of infinite life. He carries a bag of treasured secrets of heaven and earth. He is happy and content.

14. *Vanavasa* shows disdain for the Great Void and has celestial airs and a religious spirit although he is carefree and leisurely. Transcending this world, he is cheerful and peaceful.

15. *Asita* is a compassionate elder who has attained acute understanding of the universe.

16. *Pantha the Younger* is powerful, husky, and tough. He valiantly annihilates evil with his alertness and vigilance.

17. *Nantimitolo* is endowed with power that knows no bounds. He is full of valor, vigorand awe-inspiring dignity as he slays a ferocious dragon.

18. *Pindola* is infinitely resourceful, vigorous, and powerful, for he has subdued a ferocious tiger.

The arhats all have unique gifts and attributes to share, from bravery to compassion, and from absolute joy to completely content. They are each parts of one great whole. I approach employees as if they are all the different arhats; I respect the worth and dignity of each one and know that their talents and style contribute to the whole. They all have a place in the business. If they don't fit well in one area of the enterprise, they may fit better in another. If we don't accept them and empower them, they won't have their own sky to fly. And there will be conflict.

The best way to have harmony in the workplace is through a cultivation of *wu*—self-awareness. I have utilized the Kolbe Indexes/Instinct Assessment for team building—and we all know each other's scores so that we can better understand where a person is coming from and how they operate. It helps with knowing how to communicate, delegate, and resolve issues—as well as how to best use our talents. There are several other excellent assessments that can assist us in better understanding how we think, work, and communicate in comparison to others. But it is up to the leader to consciously cultivate and model a culture in which all are respected and aware that *differences don't mean deficits.*

GIVE THEM WINGS

You deserve your own sky to fly.—Lily Huang Carrier

Many leaders are not willing to trust their employees and think that they cannot learn and grow, so they will not allow them to take on responsibilities. This happens a lot with small businesses. We all have so much invested in our little enterprises, we are not going to hand over the reins to someone who could botch a job and subsequently make us look incompetent in front of clients, patients, and customers. The mind-set of "It's just easier to do it myself" creeps in, and that sets the pattern for never letting go of anything and working long hours.

I think of one of my clients who owns a local home care company. The business was growing so fast that she had to hire more certified employees to help out, but she refused to trust them to work on their own for fear that they might do something wrong, say something stupid to a patient, or otherwise make her company look bad. So she would allow these very competent employees to assist her on the job but not go it alone. But I say to her, if you can learn these skills, why can't they?

Why are you allowing fear to hold your company back from success? It reminds me of an old phrase in China: *beigong sheying,* "mistaking the reflection of a bow in the cup for a snake." A man is having a cup of tea and thinks that he sees a snake in the cup, and he jumps in fear, but it is actually the reflection of the bow hanging on the wall. You can't let the fear defeat you. Believe me, I've been there, and I know how it feels! I had created an effective risk management system, but I was fighting the shadow until I defeated the fear. Don't be ruled by imaginary fears and suspicions. Allow your employees to learn like you did and give them the authority over their projects; they will also have the responsibility to make sure it goes well.

Your employees need to have the freedom to cultivate their own *wu* and their own sense of responsibility. Sure, they may not have a financial stake in your business, but if you give them freedom, they will have pride in their accomplishments, and they will have dignity and purpose.

Daniel H. Pink notes in *Drive: The Surprising Truth about What Motivates Us* that people are not motivated by money or prizes or praise—we are seeking the rewards of having a purpose and doing a job well.[4] We all want a pleasing process for a worthwhile purpose. According to several behavioral science studies, autonomous motivation promotes greater conceptual understanding, better grades, enhanced persistence at school and in sporting activities, higher productivity, less burnout, and greater levels of psychological well-being.[5] Those efforts carry over to the workplace. Pink states, "perhaps it is time to toss the very word 'management' into the linguistic ash heap alongside 'icebox' and 'horseless carriage.' This era doesn't call for better management. It calls for a renaissance of self-direction."[6]

I agree with Pink that we are by nature curious and self-directed, but so much of that is drilled out of us in school. As a leader, I believe it is up to me to foster a sense of curiosity and autonomy in my team. We are all working together—while working differently—for the same aim. Giving what's called "autonomy support" is the key. Leaders must model their excitement for autonomy, put themselves in the shoes of the employees to see their point of view, give deep and *meaningful training, information, and feedback*, provide enough choices for the employees, over *both what to do and how to do it*, and encourage employees to take on new challenges. I liken this to the aphorism I mentioned earlier, *Baigi shitou da zajide jao*, "Pick up a stone, only to drop it on one's toes." If you feel as if you are holding the stone of your business alone, you will drop it on your toes. But when many hands are holding up the stone together, as a team and with determination and dedication, you could all hold that stone forever. That is sustainable leadership.

Set high expectations for your employees, trust them, give them the whole sky, and they will fly higher than your expectations.

HIRE SOMEONE TO RUN YOUR BUSINESS

Even though most of us nurse entrepreneurs are intensely invested in the success of our business, we can't do everything, and we aren't necessarily adept at everything. It's been said that a good rule of thumb is to hire someone who would be taking over a great portion of your own operational duties.

Mark Zuckerberg, cofounder and CEO of Facebook, was not looking for a COO, but after he met Sheryl Sandberg, a Google executive, at a conference, he realized that she should be in charge of operations. You see, he really is a software programmer and product person. In high school he built a music player, but he wasn't actually starting any businesses. In fact, he turned down multimillion-dollar offers from AOL and Microsoft, who wanted to buy his software and hire him. So in the early years of Facebook—knowing that he wasn't adept at the business side of things—he wooed Sandberg away. According to a *New York Times* article: "Ms. Sandberg has focused on building the business, expanding internationally, cultivating relationships with large advertisers and putting her polish on things like communications and public policy. That has freed Mr. Zuckerberg to focus on what he likes best: the Facebook site and its platform."[7]

Imagine how difficult it may have been for Zuckerberg to give up the reins. But if you realize that you are better equipped for employee training and patient care and want to let someone else actually run the business, that's okay!

GROWING PEOPLE

If you want one year of prosperity, grow grain. If you want ten years of prosperity, grow trees. If you want one hundred years of prosperity, grow people.—Chinese proverb

Here is something that may surprise you: new entrepreneurs often resist training and developing their staff. Because we are pressed for time and sometimes money, we find it difficult to devote the resources to showing people the ropes or sending them to workshops or conferences. I have heard entrepreneurs complain that not only is it expensive, it pulls time away from the actual work that they were hired to do, and it seems like a waste. Many worry that they will invest copious amounts of money to send staff to pay for classes or certification programs, and they fear that the employee will abandon them for a new job once they have something new on their résumé. But, we absolutely must invest in all types of training and personal development in order to transform employees and your business.

First, you must go back to that idea of cultivating a culture—a growth mind-set culture—in which learning is valued. From the moment employees come on board, you should not only train them in procedures and protocol but also provide a sound introduction and orientation regarding your growth mind-set and learning culture. Clearly communicate to staff that you expect all employees to sharpen the saw or to stay on top of their professions or fields of work. Make sure you support their efforts in this area by supplying the resources they need to accomplish these goals.

If, in the monitoring process (see chapter 10), you notice weaknesses in communications, processes, morale, or customer satisfaction, these are the opportunities for informal pullouts or learning clubs (essentially book clubs)—or formal mentorship programs, guest speakers, or in-services. They need not be expensive, but even if they are, consider it anyway.

We small-business owners worry that these investments of time and money won't get a return, so start at the end. What is the benefit that the business will experience through this development opportunity, and is it worth this investment? For example, let's say that you have promoted an especially insightful, bright, and hardworking sales representative to a team leader position, but things seem to be falling apart in her area. Oftentimes, we promote people who are adept in one position, like sales, but not in the other, such as leadership. How much would your sales improve if you sent her to a leadership coaching program? What would be the return on investment for that $1,700? It could be a hundredfold! And more importantly, she would sense your trust in her, feel more empowered, come back renewed, and be more willing to contribute to the success of the company.

Encourage your employees to research their own opportunities—more importantly, do your research and keep your ears open for new programs, speakers, workshops, and events, and reflect on rewarding development experiences in the past. Was it a retreat, a certain book, an open-source online course, a class, a professional conference, a TED talk video, or a webinar that inspired you? If these things inspired you, they will inspire your staff.

When things are going well and sales are booming, we tend to think that our energy would be better invested in increasing the good times. Remember my words of wisdom: *Ju an si wei*, "Think of danger in times of safety." The best time to develop talent is when things are running smoothly—because that is when the freshest ideas will happen and you will stay ahead of the curve. When times are tough, people tend to eliminate development programs altogether, but even when the rain is falling, these expenses should be determined by the targeted business results you want, not other budget-related factors. You should always plan for the future. Continually monitor your training and development needs to identify areas for growth. Your employees are your most important assets. Grow your people thoughtfully and strategically, and you will have years and years of prosperity.

TEAMWORK AND ELEVATOR PITCHES

A single tree does not make a forest;
a single string cannot make music.–Chinese proverb

It doesn't matter whether it's a small or large business, whether you are rich or poor. No matter how much profit you make, there is a fundamental question: how do you position yourself in relation to others? If it's better for the group, it's better for you. There is a dynamic give and take of energy.

Teamwork is not established just by establishing teams but by creating a culture of vision, transparency, growth, acceptance, playfulness, purpose, and accountability. Nothing spells disaster more than when a team member isn't pulling his/her own weight and all are pointing fingers at each other.

Too many employers allow—or even encourage—their employees to behave irresponsibly, by being absent or tardy, consistently favoring their own interests over those of their teammates or customers, failing to accept responsibilities for shortcomings, and failing to keep commitments and deadlines.

Failing to create a culture of trust and accountability—even in seemingly small matters, like leaving dirty dishes in the sink—can be a hit to productivity, prompt responsible employees to resign, and eventually cost you profits. You must employ a proactive approach. Start this before you need to; it is much harder to put that genie back in the bottle once people know that they won't be held accountable. The good news is that smaller companies have an easier time with creating a system that encourages accountability. Business gurus and authors Julie Miller and Brian Bedford note the success of the following strategies,[8] which I happen to use myself:

1. **Use an elevator pitch.** Just as you would create a pithy sales pitch for a potential customer, create a concise statement that will convince your team that a culture of personal responsibility is an important goal. "Make it a compelling pitch about how accountability will benefit us all," Miller says.[9]

2. **Write down the guidelines.** Create a document that details what you mean by accountability. It can be a fuzzy subject. Some may think they are being model employees, but they fail to see the areas in which they are not fulfilling their obligations. "That brings accountability to life," Miller says. "You might say, 'We're going to provide feedback. We're going to do what we say we will do.'"[10]

3. **Weave accountability into your organization.** Miller says that you shouldn't just announce the guidelines, print them in a handbook, and forget about them. "That's where you'll get skepticism," Miller says.[11] Instead, make it part of every facet of your organization, from hiring to training meetings, performance reviews and celebrations. Be careful not to promote or otherwise reward team members who haven't reached their goals or who have reached their goals at others' expense. Reward positive personal growth and cooperation above achievements. That will send a powerful message.

4. **Be a model of excellence.** Modeling the behavior and mind-set you expect is the best way to influence your team. Be clear that you hold the same high expectations for yourself as you do them. Follow through on your commitments, admit when you are wrong, and have what leadership expert Ronald Heifetz calls "courageous conversations."[12] When your team sees you honoring your own guidelines and modeling your decision-making process, they will then know how important it is to you—and they will do the same on their own. "Imagine a group of people sitting in a conference room trying to decide whether to ship something or not," Minda Zetlin says.[13] "If your accountability guidelines include the statement, 'We do not ship anything unless it's a quality product,' then the decision is easy."[14]

Don't worry that this will hamper your overall positive and relaxed working environment: everyone needs boundaries and guidelines keep us rooted. It doesn't mean that you can't have a Ping-Pong table set up for brainstorming, and it doesn't mean you won't have Pizza Friday; it just means that when you are engaged in playfulness you will be respecting each other as team members who are all working for the same goals.

NURTURING THE TEAM: MY TEN PILLARS OF SUPPORT

A single beam cannot support a great house.—Chinese proverb

Many employers absolutely detest the idea of nurturing their employees. They think: "I'm paying them, I praise them, and that's good enough. I'm not their mother." They may have a fear of becoming an enabler, a mushy feel-good cheerleader—which some would consider as no-no because it could cloud your vision. When I say to nurture your team, I am talking about setting in place activities and environments that nourish rather than deplete them. It isn't empty gestures, like flowers on their birthday. Meaningful structures and processes encourage growth, harmony, a sense of purpose, pride in one's work, and these structures create an overall safe place in which to be one's authentic self—and thrive!

My ten pillars of nurturing your team players are

1. Being open and accessible
2. Honoring their time
3. Creating space and time for self-care and reflection
4. Being inclusive and accepting
5. Being humble
6. Praising their efforts
7. Honestly assessing their work
8. Supporting their goals
9. Respecting their personal lives
10. Having fun

These are simple precepts, really.

1. **Being open and accessible.** I make myself available to my people with an open-door policy. If the door is open, come on in! They are encouraged to share everything laterally as well as up the chain. It's important that I calmly

and actively listen without jumping to conclusions or teaching a lesson. People need to be heard and validated. I also use anonymous feedback surveys, free on surveymonkey.com. Then I respond to or act on feedback or both. But it is important to note that I don't always fix problems; I may just advise. At problem-solving meetings, everyone on the team can contribute, and it is important for them to know that they have a say into what happens organizationally. If someone has a grievance about someone else on the team, it is important that I do not participate in triangulation, in which one person complains about another in hopes that I will mend the situation. This forces people into a triangle of victim, persecutor, and savior, which is a very unhealthy model of communication in any organization. My advice is for the person with a grievance to go back and open an effective communication with the other person. If the two people need help on how to effectively and fairly resolve the issue after that, I certainly can be of help and support.

2. **Honoring their time.** I know I am getting something very precious from my team staff: their time. I make efficiency a priority: meetings are well planned, work is streamlined using the correct channels, we avoid redundancy, and I reward them for the extra time they spend at work. I also encourage off-site work and unconventional hours, when appropriate. They receive fair amounts of personal days, vacation days, and sick days. They could be working someplace else, but they chose to work on my team. I will always honor that.

3. **Creating space and time for self-care and reflection.** While you can alter the health of your own mind through healthy mental habits such as sleep (lack of sleep costs the United States an estimated $63 billion each year in lost productivity),[15] exercise, and meditation, you can also model healthy self-care and development of *wu* by creating environments and opportunities conducive to positive habits. Some ideas are completely free. You can also encourage environmental changes with houseplants, clean work areas, calming music, aromatherapy, and photos of loved ones or even pets—all of which are proven to boost performance as well.[16] Some other ideas are healthy snacks in the fridge, group charity fun runs, healthy catered lunches, and encouraging volunteer activities, which are proven to boost spirits. Also encourage employees to assist with office design.

4. **Being inclusive and accepting.** I've mentioned the importance of creating a culture where all are treated as arhats and valued for their uniqueness. But your employees must understand how that is accomplished. First of all, we make sure to include all voices in meetings (see chapter 10 for the process-observer role). Everybody counts, and everybody knows they count. We also have rules of communication. We don't gab or gossip; we avoid judging each other; we keep things professional. And while we may share some personal celebrations such as births, weddings, and vacations, we avoid topics that may be too personal. Procedural complaints are welcome at meetings, but personal grievances should be handled at the individual level (see the number one pillar above). We don't need to agree with everyone's decisions or beliefs in order to succeed as a team. In fact, I would call being overly concerned with differences another form of picking up the sesames. If there is a true concern—perhaps, say, someone is not the right temperament for a certain position—that only means that they should consider a different position within the organization or that we can work together to develop their talents. When employees opt to judge or exclude each other, it is because they are afraid. They are really sending a sign of fear or feelings of low self-worth. This needs to be addressed quickly, because a team will quickly fall apart when all are not accepted and valued.

5. **Being humble.** I don't believe that I am any better, wiser, or smarter than any of my employees, and that shows in everything I do. I decenter myself in meetings by sitting next to everyone else (like a guide on the side rather than a sage on the stage). I don't have the nicest office or furniture in the building. In fact, I remember during one period of rapid expansion squeezing a chair next to the printer and file cabinets for quite a while— just so others could have the space they deserved. Furthermore, I may have seen what my people's struggles, challenges, or personal lives are like, but I cannot judge them or their motivations. I can only see the light in them. My team knows how much the business means to me, and they all deserve my admiration and my deepest gratitude and humility. It is only as a team that we all succeed.

I hope you learned the secret from this Monkey King's lesson like I did.

The Buddha said: "I will make a deal with you. If you can somersault out of my right palm in one somersault, then I will let the Jade Emperor give you his power; otherwise, you will have to cultivate for thousands of years on Earth."

Looking at the Buddha's palm, which was no more than a foot in length, Monkey King smiled to himself and hastily said: "Are you sure you can handle this?" The Buddha said: "Sure, sure."

So Monkey King stood in the middle of the Tathagata's right palm, feeling that the palm was no bigger than a lotus leaf. He did one somersault and kept moving forward until he saw five huge pillars. He had surmised that he had reached the end of the Heavens and to prove his trail, he urinated at the bottom of the first pillar, pulled out one of his hairs and said: "Change!" He then changed the hair into a big brush and wrote on the middle pillar the words "The great Sage as high as Heaven visited here."

He returned to the center of the Buddha's right palm with another somersault and shouted to the Buddha: "I left and returned; you should now let the Jade Emperor give me his power." The Buddha said: "You Monkey, do you know that you are still in my palm?" Monkey King said: "You just don't know that I went to the end of the Heavens and found five red pillars there. I left a sign there. Do you dare to go with me to check?" The Buddha said: "There is no need for me to go and check; you just look down and you will see." Monkey King looked and found that on the middle finger of the Buddha's right hand, there was a line of words: "The great Sage as high as Heaven visited here." And there was also a strong smell of urine in the Buddha's hand.

Monkey King was very surprised and said: "How can this be? I wrote these words on a pillar that supports Heaven, but how can it be on your finger? No, I don't believe it. It is impossible."

Hahaha! I can't help laughing every time I read it! I hope you get the message: no matter how good we are, there is always someone better. Cultivate Monkey King's mind-set, but be humble!

6. **Praising their efforts.** Our team members must be praised—both privately and publicly—for their achievements and hard work. We avoid praising innate qualities such as being smart and talented, but instead praise effort! One of my favorite ways of doing this is during our weekly team meetings. We go around and answer the question, who helped me this week? It is a great opportunity for genuine peer-to-peer praise. Other fun ideas for public praise are to use the company website to highlight employee's achievements, include an item in the company newsletter,

or have a monthly hot seat, when an employee sits in a chair and we all come up with as many positive contributions and achievements as we can think of. Remember, no qualities like pretty or bright. On my own, I give positive feedback with a quick call or email, a special handwritten note, or a gesture of appreciation from the team, such as a gift to an employee's favorite charity or a gift related to their favorite pastime. It shows that you care enough to learn about them outside of work. I also make sure that we keep track of achievements as they happen in their portfolio so that we can honor their cumulative achievements as well. One last thing about showing your appreciation: truly show you care with nonverbal communication as well, such as maintaining eye contact, positioning yourself square to their body, sitting on their level in meetings, or smiling when walking by their desk. When you care about employees, it will show.

7. **Honestly assessing their work.** When conducting periodic evaluations of your employees, be sure to be completely candid in your assessments. Always start with a positive, then share an opportunity for growth, then end with another positive. You will have some difficult conversations, to be sure. Psychologist Ronald Heifetz says that during these "courageous conversations . . . we must engage above and below the neck . . . courage requires all of you: heart mind, spirit, and guts."[17] It is essential that employees be grounded in their reality. Our hope is that they will know what they could improve on when they write their self-assessment because they have been practicing self-awareness and mindfulness, but quite possibly you will be holding up a mirror to something that they have never realized about themselves—or, conversely, realizing that they are not escaping a known pattern. We owe them honesty. An employee evaluation is also an excellent time to talk about how they are realizing the goals and vision of the organization. As the wise sages said, "An oil lamp becomes brighter after trimming; a truth becomes clearer after being discussed."

8. **Respecting their personal lives.** I truly respect my employees' privacy, but on the other hand, I truly care for them. My mantra is to follow a balanced path: be involved, not invasive. If employees volunteer information, I certainly will address an issue, but sometimes it can be difficult. One employee, for instance, had a miscarriage. Such a delicate situation. Private

condolences were in order after she disclosed it, and it was important to make sure she had support from her family and community. I have to be careful to not assume an inappropriately close relationship to my employees—even if, as a nurse, I'd love to! In addition to being sensitive to private issues, it is wise to also understand the value of a work-life balance. I model this priority myself. As they say, we should be working to live, not living to work.

9. **Having fun.** What would a Monkey King entrepreneur do without having fun? There are the traditional ways of having fun: company outings, annual picnics, softball and bowling leagues, team-building and ice-breaker games, casual Fridays, and birthday celebrations, but that is nothing these days! How about some really fun ones? Like live-action role-playing games, theme days (The '80s, Superhero, Cowboy, for example), treasure hunts, Office Olympics (as on *The Office*), trivia contests, fake office awards (remember the Dundies?), or nontraditional team-building games like "Two Truths and a Lie." Encourage the team to come up with its own creative ideas and plan the events. There is no better way to boost morale than a little levity.

IN THE END, SUPPORT

In the end, all of the frameworks we have in place to empower our employees will fall flat unless they have a deep and profound knowledge that they are fundamentally supported.

Supporting their goals. The other side of an employee evaluation is encouraging them to outline their personal and professional goals—and supporting them in this. They have been supporting your company's goals; now it's time for you to support theirs. Try to get to the essence of your employees. Who are they? What do they need to grow? How can you help them arrive at this growth independently and on their own terms? Help them to create a road map to achieve their professional goals; they truly may not know how to get from here to there. It is important to encourage lateral moves within the company. Young people—millennials—may still be trying on positions to find the right fit. Moving laterally helps employees try something new, which builds their energy and enthusiasm for the vision of the company.

Chapter 12

Using Your W.I.T.

TRANSFORMING FROM MONKEY TO MONKEY KING

THE STORY OF MONKEY KING is one of an intrepid, courageous monkey who takes on the entire world—just like an entrepreneur! We think big, have great confidence, and take on every challenge fearlessly. We must use our W.I.T. to know how to claim the respect, freedom, and prosperity we deserve.

W—Willingness. You must be willing to let go of your cycle of defeat, your fears, and your fixed roles. You must cultivate a willingness to believe in your own value, to change your habits, and to commit to self-care. Every time I look back at the challenges I took on, I remember that I had tons of fear and thoughts. But it's not the fear that's important—it's the awareness and resilience to be able to confront the fear. Forgive yourself for the mistakes you've made and for your doubts and fears. You will want to run away from your shadow; accept that it's your shadow. Transform the fearful or negative force into a powerful force.

I—Insight. Reflect on your inner self (*wu*), follow your instincts (*zhijue*), and be aware of your impact on the world (*zhong yong*). When cultivating insight, the goal is to reveal the optimal quality of your life, become self-aware, and rebuild a relationship with yourself, your business, and the world around you. It is also to attract what you are focused on. Through mindfulness, singleness of purpose, focusing on goals, and meditation, you will gain the understanding that you already possessed the skills and tools to optimally serve others as a nurse entrepreneur. We know that the dominating thoughts of our minds attract circumstances that reflect those thoughts to complete our vision.

T—Talent. Use what you've acquired and acquire more! Continue to develop professionally, cultivate your leadership and vision, create allies, draw out team members, and think of how to use your gifts for the greater good. I think of the Elephant Trunk Hill, the Seven Star Park, the Ling Canal, and the Nine Horses Cliff—which all have sustaining legacies to this day. What you do in this moment with your talents will impact generations to come.

I believe that if you have a dream, and have the vision to believe in your dream, you can transform and create the life you dreamed of.

Conclusion:

Bringing The Wisdom

....

To know the road ahead, ask those coming back.

—Chinese proverb

....

SO MANY PEOPLE BELIEVE THAT you pick one career, and you stick with it, that life is a straight line of building, and that we build on one choice that we made when we were in our teens or twenties. But this is not true. We are a beautiful tapestry. All of our experiences in our personal and professional lives—everything from heartache to hobbies to hospital work—create who we really are and make us strong and wise. We bring this wisdom and strength to our greater purpose.

I think of Monkey King's journey to his purpose in life. At the beginning, he learned some magic (*gongfu*), had some amazing adventures, and eventually got in some big troubles—especially when he was stuck under the Five Finger Mountain for 500 years. These adventures did not make him a hero.

In the end, he found his purpose by using all of his skills, strength, and wisdom to help the entire team retrieve the sutras from the west—and bring enlightenment and peace to all. He found that his real calling was more important than his early adventures and was incredibly meaningful for billions of people for generations to come. My hope is that you have learned from the deepest secret of Monkey King's life how you, too, can rely on all you already have to embark on your own hero's journey—your own entrepreneurship.

Notes

Chapter 1: Bullying, Babies, Bladders, and Burnout

1. Atefi, N., Abdullah, K. L., Wong, L. P., & Mazlom, R. (2014). Factors influencing registered nurses perception of their overall job satisfaction: A qualitative study: Factors influencing nurses job satisfaction. *International Nursing Review*, 61(3), 352–360. doi:10.1111/inr.12112

2. Yu, M., & Kang, K. J. (2016). Factors affecting turnover intention for new graduate nurses in three transition periods for job and work environment satisfaction. *The Journal of Continuing Education in Nursing*, 47(3), 120. Retrieved June 20, 2016, from http://dx.doi.org/doi:10.3928/00220124-20160218-08

3. Hooper, C., Craig, J., Janvrin, D. R., Wetsel, M. A., & Reimels, E. (2010). Compassion satisfaction, burnout, and compassion fatigue among emergency nurses compared with nurses in other selected inpatient specialties. *Journal of Emergency Nursing*, 36(5), 420–427. Retrieved from http://dx.doi.org/10.1016/j.jen.2009.11.027

4. American Sociological Association (ASA). (2014, August 19). Nurses driven mainly by a desire to help others are more likely to burn out. *ScienceDaily*. Retrieved April 5, 2016, from www.sciencedaily.com/releases/2014/08/140819082918.htm

5. American Holistic Nurses Association. (2015). Holistic stress management for nurses. Retrieved April 5, 2016, from http://www.ahna.org/Resources/Stress-Management

6. *Scrubs Magazine*. (2016, February 10). Recognizing & coping with nursing burnout. Retrieved April 5, 2016, from http://scrubsmag.com/recognizing-coping-with-nursing-burnout

7. Gupta, S. (2015, September 14). Why America's nurses are burning out. Everyday Health Media, LLC. Retrieved April 5, 2016, from http://www.everydayhealth.com/news/why-americas-nurses-are-burning-out

8. Vitale, Susan Ann, Varrone-Ganesh, Jessica, & Vu, Melisa. (2015). Nurses working the night shift: Impact on home, family and social life. *Journal of Nursing Education and Practice*. Retrieved April 5, 2016, from http://www.sciedu.ca/journal/index.php/jnep/article/viewFile/7294/4497

9. *Nursing Management*. (2015). Shift work can lead to obesity and diabetes, figures show. Retrieved June 20, 2016, from http://dx.doi.org/10.7748/nm.21.9.7.s6

10. Ibid.

11. Ibid.

12. Rogers, A. E., Hwang, W., Scott, L. D., Aiken, L. H., & Dinges, D. F. (2004). The working hours of hospital staff nurses and patient safety. *Health Affairs*, 23(4), 202–212. doi:10.1377/hlthaff.23.4.202

13. Hirsch A., A. J., Park, J. E., Adhami, N., Sirounis, D., Tholin, H., Dodek, P., & Ayas, N. (2014). Impact of work schedules on sleep duration of critical care nurses. *American Journal of Critical Care: An Official Publication*, American Association of Critical-Care Nurses, 23(4), 290. Retrieved from http://doi.org/10.4037/ajcc2014876

14. Jacobsen, R. Widespread understaffing of nurses increases risk to patients. (2015, July 14). *Scientific American*. Retrieved April 5, 2016, from http://www.scientificamerican.com/article/widespread-understaffing-of-nurses-increases-risk-to-patients

15. Tuten, T. (2012, September 26). Reducing nurse burnout: A win-win solution. *Huffington Post*. Retrieved April 5, 2016, from http://www.huffingtonpost.com/tera-tuten/reducing-nurse-burnout_b_1916350.html

16. Ibid.

17. Aiken, L. H., Cimiotti, J. P., Sloane, D. M., Smith, H. L., Flynn, L., & Neff, D. F. (2011). The effects of nurse staffing and nurse education on patient deaths in hospitals with different nurse work environments. *Medical Care*, 49(12), 1047–1053. Retrieved from http://doi.org/10.1097/MLR.0b013e3182330b6e

18. Brock, D., Abu-Rish, E., Chiu, C., Hammer, D., Wilson, S., Vorvick, L., Ziegler, B. (2013). Interprofessional education in team communication: Working together to improve patient safety. *BMJ Quality & Safety*, 22(5), 414. Retrieved June 20, 2016, from http://doi.org/10.1136/bmjqs-2012-000952

19. Walrafen, N., Brewer, M., Mulvenon, C. (2012). Sadly caught up in the moment: An exploration of horizontal violence. *Nurse Economics.* Retrieved April 5, 2016, from http://www.medscape.com/viewarticle/760015_3

20. Cleary, M., Walter, G., Sayers, J., Lopez, V., & Hungerford, C. (2015). Arrogance in the workplace: Implications for mental health nurses. *Issues in Mental Health Nursing*, 36(4), 266–271. Retrieved June 20, 2016, from http://doi.org/10.3109/01612840.2014.955934

21. Ibid.

22. Wood, D. Study finds nurses need more work-life balance. AMN Healthcare, Inc. Retrieved April 5, 2016, from http://www.travelnursing.com/news-and-features/news-detail/study-finds-nurses-need-more-work-life-balance/31238

23. Ibid.

24. Vickie Malazzo Institute. (2014). "Are you way too stressed out?" Survey results: An assessment of the stress levels of nurses in the United States. Retrieved April 5, 2016, from http://www.legalnurse.com/wp-content/uploads/2014/06/RN-Stress-Survey-Results-2014-VickieMilazzoInstitute.pdf

25. Tunnah, K., Jones, A., & Johnstone, R. (2012). Stress in hospice at home nurses: A qualitative study of their experiences of their work and wellbeing. *International Journal Of Palliative Nursing*, 18(6), 283–289. Retrieved June 20, 2016, from http://doi.org/10.4236/ojn.2014.42009

26. Toh, S. G., Ang, E., & Devi, M. K. (2012). Systematic review on the relationship between the nursing shortage and job satisfaction, stress and burnout levels among nurses in oncology/hematology settings. *International Journal of Evidence-Based Healthcare*, 10(2), 126–141. doi:10.1111/j.1744-1609.2012.00271

27. Jenkins, R., & Elliott, P. (2004). Stressors, burnout and social support: Nurses in acute mental health settings. *Journal of Advanced Nursing*, 48(6), 622–631. doi:10.1111/j.1365-2648.2004.03240.x

28. Browning, L., Ryan, C., Thomas, S., Greenberg, M., & Rolniak, S. (2007). Nursing specialty and burnout. *Psychology, Health, and Medicine*, 12(2), 248–254. doi: 10.1016/j.ridd.2011.01.025

29. Gamecock 73. (2013, October 1). I didn't burnout, I went up in a great big ball of flames . . . Allnurses.com. Retrieved April 5, 2016, from http://allnurses.com/general-nursing-discussion/i-didnt-burnout-880797.html

30. Jennings, B. M. (2008). Work stress and burnout among nurses: Role of the work environment and working conditions. Hughes, R. G., editor. *Patient safety and quality: An evidence-based handbook for nurses.* Agency for Healthcare Research and Quality (US); Chapter 26. Retrieved April 5, 2016, from http://www.ncbi.nlm.nih.gov/books/NBK2668

31. Vickie Malazzo Institute. (2014). "Are you way too stressed out?" Survey results: An assessment of the stress levels of nurses in the United States. Retrieved April 5, 2016, from http://www.legalnurse.com/wp-content/uploads/2014/06/RN-Stress-Survey-Results-2014-VickieMilazzoInstitute.pdf

32. Ibid.

33. Jennings, B. M. (2008). Work stress and burnout among nurses: Role of the work environment and working conditions. Hughes, R. G., editor. *Patient safety and quality: An evidence-based handbook for nurses.* Agency for Healthcare Research and Quality (US); Chapter 26. Retrieved April 5, 2016, from http://www.ncbi.nlm.nih.gov/books/NBK2668

34. Seppa, N. (2015). The mess that is stress: Chronic angst triggers a slew of changes that harm long-term health. Science Service, Inc. doi:10.1002/scin.2015.187005017

35. American Nurses Association. (2011). 2011 ANA health and safety survey. Retrieved April 5, 2016, from http://www.nursingworld.org/MainMenuCategories/WorkplaceSafety/Healthy-Work-Environment/Work-Environment/2011-HealthSafetySurvey.html

36. Katie, B. (2015, August 14). Byron Katie Blog. Retrieved April 5, 2016, from http://www.byronkatie.com/2015/08/stress-is-an

37. Furillo, J. (n.d.). Student debt hurts nursing students, too. New York State Nurses Association. Retrieved April 5, 2016 from http://www.nysna.org/student-debt-hurts-nursing-students-too#.VwRkwaQrLIV

38. Vickie Malazzo Institute. (2014). "Are you way too stressed out?" Survey results: An assessment of the stress levels of nurses in the United States. Retrieved April 5, 2016, from http://www.legalnurse.com/wp-content/uploads/2014/06/RN-Stress-Survey-ResultsResult-2014-VickieMilazzoInstitute.pdf

Chapter 2: So You Want To Be A Nurse Entrepreneur?

1. Wilson, A., Whitaker, N., & Whitford, D. (2012). Rising to the challenge of health care reform with entrepreneurial and intrapreneurial nursing initiatives. *Online Journal of Issues in Nursing*, 17(2), F1. Retrieved April 6, 2016, from http://nursingworld.org/MainMenuCategories/ANAMarketplace/ANAPeriodicals/OJIN/TableofContents/Vol-17-2012/No2-May-2012/Rising-to-the-Challenge-of-Reform.html

2. International Council of Nurses. (2004). Guidelines on the nurse entre/intrapreneur providing nursing service. Retrieved April 7, 2016, from http://www.ipnig.ca/education/Guidelines-NurseEntre-ICN.pdf

3. Bureau of Labor Statistics. (2016, March 30). Occupational employment and wages, May 2015. Retrieved April 7, 2016, from http://www.bls.gov/oes/current/oes291141.htm

4. Den Hollander, K. (2013, Oct. 1). Creative ideas for self-employed nurse careers. National Association of Orthopaedic Nurses. Retrieved April 6, 2016, from http://www.orthonurse.org/p/bl/et/blogaid=525

5. Wilson, A., Whitaker, N., & Whitford, D. (2012). Rising to the challenge of health care reform with entrepreneurial and intrapreneurial nursing initiatives. *Online Journal of Issues in Nursing*, 17(2), F1. Retrieved April 6, 2016, from http://nursingworld.org/MainMenuCategories/ANAMarketplace/ANAPeriodicals/OJIN/TableofContents/Vol-17-2012/No2-May-2012/Rising-to-the-Challenge-of-Reform.html

Chapter 3: The Deepest Secret Revealed

1. AMN Healthcare, Inc. (2015). 2015 Survey of registered nurses: Viewpoints on retirement, education and emerging roles. Retrieved April 6, 2016, from http://www.amnhealthcare.com/uploadedFiles/MainSite/Content/Workforce_Solutions/2015_Survey_Registered_Nurses_FOR_WEB_SingPage.pdf

2. Heifetz, R. A., Grashow, A., & Linsky, M. (2009). *The practice of adaptive leadership: Tools and tactics for changing your organization and the world.* Boston: Harvard Business Press.

3. Pink, Daniel. (2009). *Drive: The surprising truth about what motivates us and why.* New York: Riverhead Books.

4. Ibid.

5. Rosten, L. (n.d.). Leo Rosten Quotes. Goodreads, Inc. Retrieved April 7, 2016, from https://www.goodreads.com/author/quotes/59780.Leo_Rosten

6. Dweck, C. S. (2008). *Mindset: The new psychology of success.* Ballantine Books trade paperback edition. New York: Ballantine Books.

7. Ibid.

8. Ibid

9. Ibid.

10. Ibid.

11. Ibid.

12. Ibid.

13. Dweck, C. (2016). Mindset for business & leadership. Mindset. Retrieved April 6, 2016, from http://mindsetonline.com/howmindsetaffects/businessleadership/index.html

14. Ibid.

15. Caprino, K. (2012, May 23). 10 lessons I learned from Sara Blakely that you won't hear in business school. *Forbes.* Retrieved April 6, 2016, from http://www.forbes.com/sites/kathycaprino/2012/05/23/10-lessons-i-learned-from-sara-blakely-that-you-wont-hear-in-business-school/#76c49b1a7442

16. Cuddy, A. (2015) *Presence: Bringing your boldest self to your biggest challenges.* New York: Little, Brown and Company.

17. Pausch, Randy. (uploaded 2011). *The last lecture*. Retrieved April 6, 2016, from https://www.youtube.com/watch?v=j7zzQpvoYcQ

18. Woolf, V. (1921). *Monday or Tuesday*. New York: Harcourt, Brace and Company. 1999. Bartlby.com. Retrieved April 6, 2016, from www.bartleby.com/85/.

19. Williamson, M. (1992). *A return to love: Reflections on the Principles of "A course in miracles."* New York: HarperCollins.

20. Shepard, A. (2014). *The Monkey King: A superhero tale of China*. Olympia, WA: Skyhook Press.

Chapter 4: More Than Monkeying Around

1. Jordan, M. (n.d.). BrainyQuote.com. Retrieved April 9, 2016, http://www.brainyquote.com/quotes/quotes/m/michaeljor385092.html

2. Hill, N. (1937). *Think and grow rich: Teaching, for the first time, the famous Andrew Carnegie formula for money-making, based upon the thirteen proven steps to riches.* 2011 edition. Thinking, Inc., Media.

3. Simmons, R. (2014, June 15). *Super soul Sunday*. Winfrey, O. OWN.

Chapter 5: What to Play?

1. Mullahy, C. M. (2010). *The case manager's handbook*. 4th edition. Sudbury, MA: Jones and Bartlett.

2. Weiner, L. J. (2016, Jan. 4). 2016 Healthcare Staffing Trends. Health Leaders Media. Retrieved April 11, 2016, from http://www.healthleadersmedia.com/hr/2016-healthcare-staffing-trends?page=0percent2C2

3. Wilson, A., Whitaker, N., & Whitford, D. (2012). Rising to the challenge of health care reform with entrepreneurial and intrapreneurial nursing initiatives. *Online Journal of Issues in Nursing*, 17(2), F1. Retrieved April 6, 2016, from http://nursingworld.org/MainMenuCategories/ANAMarketplace/ANAPeriodicals/OJIN/TableofContents/Vol-17-2012/No2-May-2012/Rising-to-the-Challenge-of-Reform.html

4. ANA Staff. (2015, Nov.). 4 health care trends that will affect American nurses. American Nurses Association. Retrieved April 9, 2016 from http://nursingworld.org/MainMenuCategories/Career-Center/Resources/4-Health-Care-Trends-That-Will-Affect-American-Nurses.html

5. United States Census. The baby boom cohort in the United States: 2012–2060. Retrieved April 9, 2016, from https://www.census.gov/prod/2014pubs/p25-1141.pdf

6. Administration on Aging. (n.d.). Aging statistics. Administration for Community Living. Retrieved April 8, 2016, from http://www.aoa.acl.gov/aging_statistics/index.aspx

7. United States Census. The baby boom cohort in the United States: 2012–2060. Retrieved April 9, 2016, from https://www.census.gov/prod/2014pubs/p25-1141.pdf

8. United States Centers for Disease Control. (2015). Heart disease facts. Retrieved April 8, 2016, from http://www.cdc.gov/heartdisease/facts.htm

9. United States Centers for Disease Control. (2015). Leading causes of death. Retrieved April 8, 2016, from http://www.cdc.gov/nchs/fastats/leading-causes-of-death.htm

10. Ibid.

11. Brown, B. (2015). Top 7 healthcare trends and challenges from our financial expert. HealthCatalyst. Retrieved April 9, 2016, from https://www.healthcatalyst.com/top-healthcare-trends-challenges

12. DeVore, S. (2015, Dec. 30). Six big trends to watch in health care for 2016. *Health Affairs Blog*. Retrieved April 9, 2016, from http://healthaffairs.org/blog/2015/12/30/six-big-trends-to-watch-in-health-care-for-2016

13. Ibid.

14. Brown, B. (2015). Top 7 healthcare trends and challenges from our financial expert. HealthCatalyst. Retrieved April 9, 2016, from https://www.healthcatalyst.com/top-healthcare-trends-challenges

15. Word Health Organization. (2016). World health day 2016: WHO calls for global action to halt rise in and improve care for people with diabetes. Retrieved April 8, 2016, from http://www.who.int/mediacentre/news/releases/2016/world-health-day/en

16. United States Centers for Disease Control. (2015). 2014 national diabetes statistics report. Retrieved April 9, 2106, from http://www.cdc.gov/diabetes/data/statistics/2014statisticsreport.html

17. Brown, B. (2015). Top 7 healthcare trends and challenges from our financial expert. HealthCatalyst. Retrieved April 9, 2016, from https://www.healthcatalyst.com/top-healthcare-trends-challenges

18. ANA Staff. (2015, Nov.). 4 health care trends that will affect American nurses. American Nurses Association. Retrieved April 9, 2016, from http://nursingworld.org/MainMenuCategories/Career-Center/Resources/4-Health-care-Trends-That-Will-Affect-American-Nurses.html

19. DeVore, S. (2015, Dec. 30). Six big trends to watch in health care for 2016. *Health Affairs Blog*. Retrieved April 9, 2016 http://healthaffairs.org/blog/2015/12/30/six-big-trends-to-watch-in-health-care-for-2016

20. Mullahy, C. M. (2010). *The case manager's handbook*. 4th edition.. Sudbury, MA: Jones and Bartlett.

21. Brown, B. (2015). Top 7 healthcare trends and challenges from our financial expert. HealthCatalyst. Retrieved April 9, 2016, from https://www.healthcatalyst.com/top-healthcare-trends-challenges

22. Weiner, L. J. (2016, Jan. 4) 2016 Healthcare Staffing Trends. Health Leaders Media. Retrieved April 9, 2016, from http://www.healthleadersmedia.com/hr/2016-healthcare-staffing-trends?page=0 percent2C2

23. DeVore, S. (2015, Dec. 30). Six big trends to watch in health care for 2016. *Health Affairs Blog*. Retrieved April 9, 2016, http://healthaffairs.org/blog/2015/12/30/six-big-trends-to-watch-in-health-care-for-2016

24. ANA Staff. (2015, Nov.). 4 health care trends that will affect American nurses. American Nurses Association. Retrieved April 9, 2016, from http://nursingworld.org/MainMenuCategories/Career-Center/Resources/4-Health-care-Trends-That-Will-Affect-American-Nurses.html

25. Center for Strategic and International Studies. (2013). Selected notifiable disease rates and number of new cases: United States, selected years 1950–2011. Infectious diseases. Retrieved April 9, 2016, from http://www.smartglobalhealth.org/issues/entry/infectious-disease

26. United States Centers for Disease Control. (2013). Selected notifiable disease rates and number of new cases: United States, selected years 1950–2011. Retrieved April 9, 2016, from http://www.cdc.gov/nchs/data/hus/2013/039.pdf

27. United States Centers for Disease Control. (2015). Office of financial resources FY 2015 assistance snapshot. Retrieved April 9, 2016, from http://www.cdc.gov/funding/documents/fy2015/fy-2015-ofr-assistance-snapshot.pdf

28. United States Department of Health and Human Services. Prevention and public health fund. Retrieved April 9, 2016 from http://www.hhs.gov/open/prevention

29. United States Centers for Disease Control. (2015). Heart disease facts. Retrieved April 8, 2016 from http://www.cdc.gov/heartdisease/facts.htm

30. Administration on Aging. (n.d.) Aging statistics. Administration for Community Living. Retrieved April 8, 2016, from http://www.aoa.acl.gov/aging_statistics/index.aspx

31. United States Centers for Disease Control. (2015). 2014 national diabetes statistics report. Retrieved April 9, 2106, from http://www.cdc.gov/diabetes/data/statistics/2014statisticsreport.html

32. Hooper, C., Craig, J., Janvrin, D. R., Wetsel, M. A., & Reimels, E. (2010). Compassion satisfaction, burnout, and compassion fatigue among emergency nurses compared with nurses in other selected inpatient specialties. *Journal of Emergency Nursing, 36*(5), 420–427. Retrieved April 8, 2016, from http://dx.doi.org/10.1016/j.jen.2009.11.027

33. National Center for Complementary and Integrative Health. (2016, March 16). Complementary, alternative, or integrative health: What's in a name? (2015). Retrieved April 8, 2016, from https://nccih.nih.gov/health/integrative-health

34. Ibid.

35. Natural Healers. (n.d.). Natural health career statistics. Retrieved April 8, 2016, from http://www.naturalhealers.com/natural-health-career-statistics

36. National Center for Complementary and Integrative Health. (2015, Sept. 9). NIH awards nearly $35 million to research natural products. Retrieved June 20, 2016, from https://nccih.nih.gov/news/press/09092015

37. US Department of Health and Human Services. (2015). Prevention and public health fund. Retrieved April 8, 2016, from http://www.hhs.gov/open/prevention/index.html

38. Natural Healers. (n.d.). Natural health career statistics. Retrieved April 8, 2016, from http://www.naturalhealers.com/natural-health-career-statistics

39. National Nurses in Business Association. (n.d.). Nursing agency owner. Retrieved April 8, 2016, from https://nnbanow.com/nursing-agency-owner

40. Bureau of Labor Statistics, U.S. Department of Labor (2016). Occupational outlook handbook, 2016–17 edition, Registered nurses. Retrieved April 13, 2016, from http://www.bls.gov/ooh/health care/registered-nurses.htm

41. PricewaterhouseCoopers. (2009) Pharma 2020: Marketing the future—which path will you take? Retrieved June 20, 2016, from http://www.pwc.com/gx/en/pharma-life-sciences/pdf/ph2020-marketing.pdf

42. Debelak, D. (2002). I needed that. *Entrepreneur.* Retrieved April 8, 2016, from https://www.entrepreneur.com/article/51140

43. Bunger, J. D. (2008). Nurse entrepreneurs. *Nebraska Nursing News.* Retrieved June 20, 2016, from http://dhhs.ne.gov/publichealth/Documents/NNfall2008.pdf

44. Ibid.

45. Nanobugs. (2011). Cleaning professionals. Retrieved April 10, 2016, from http://nanobugs.com/cleaning-professionals

46. Fitzpatrick, J. J., and Ea, E. E. (2012). *201 careers in nursing.* New York: Springer Publishing.

47. Florida Nurse Practitioner Network. (2013). Jean Aertker DNP, ARNP-BC, COHN-S, FAANP, wins AANP board of directors post. Retrieved April 10, 2016, from https://fnpn.enpnetwork.com/nurse-practitioner-news/19501-jean-aertker-dnp-arnp-bc-cohn-s-faanp-wins-aanp-board-of-directors-post

48. Bunger, J. D. (2008). Nurse entrepreneurs. *Nebraska Nursing News.* Retrieved June 20, 2016, from http://dhhs.ne.gov/publichealth/Documents/NNfall2008.pdf

49. Bunger, J. D. (2008). Nurse entrepreneurs. *Nebraska Nursing News.* Retrieved June 20, 2016, from http://dhhs.ne.gov/publichealth/Documents/NNfall2008.pdf

50. SerRobCo, Inc. Importance of body piercing removal kit. Retrieved April 10, 2016, from http://www.serrobco.com/

51. UCEDC. (n.d.). R.N. becomes holistic health entrepreneur with UCEDC help. Retrieved April 10, 2016, from https://ucedc.com/client/registered-nurse-becomes-holistic-health-entrepreneur-with-ucedc-assistance

52. Cleansing Waters, LLC. Cleansing Waters. Retrieved April 10, 2016, from http://cleansingwatersllc.com

53. Grensing-Pophal, L. (2012, April 25). Nurse entrepreneurs. Advanced Health Network. Retrieved April 10, 2016, from http://nursing.advanceweb.com/Features/Articles/Nurse-Entrepreneurs.aspx

54. Firstlight Homecare Franchising, LLC. (2016). From nursing to in-home care: One franchise owner's experience. Retrieved April 10, 2016, from http://www.firstlighthomecare.com/e/v3/9

55. Firstlight Homecare Franchising, LLC. (2016). Where do you need service? Retrieved April 10, 2016, from http://www.firstlighthomecare.com

56. SerRobCo, Inc. Importance of body piercing removal kit. Retrieved April 10, 2016, from http://www.serrobco.com/

57. Grensing-Pophal, L. (2012, April 25). Nurse entrepreneurs. Advanced Health Network Retrieved April 10, 2016 from http://nursing.advanceweb.com/Features/Articles/Nurse-Entrepreneurs.aspx

58. VeinInnovations. (2016). Locations. Retrieved April 10, 2016, from http://veininnovations.com

Chapter 6: My Expertise

1. Mullahy, C. M. (2010). *The case manager's handbook.* 4th edition. Sudbury, MassA: Jones and Bartlett.

2. Commission for Case Management Certification. (n.d.). Growing trend: Case management certification desired [and paid for] by more employers. CCMC Issue Brief, Vol 1, Iss. 1. Retrieved June 20, 2016, from https://ccmcertification.org/sites/default/files/downloads/2011/3.%20 Growing%20trend,%20case%20managers%20desired,%20volume%20 1,%20issue%201.pdf

3. Mullahy, C. M. (2010). *The case manager's handbook.* 4th edition. Sudbury, MA: Jones and Bartlett.

4. Commission for Case Management Certification. (n.d.). Growing trend: Case management certification desired [and paid for] by more employers. CCMC Issue Brief, Vol 1, Iss. 1. Retrieved June 20, 2016, from https://ccmcertification.org/sites/default/files/downloads/2011/3.%20 Growing%20trend,%20case%20managers%20desired,%20volume%20 1,%20issue%201.pdf

5. Mullahy, C. M. (2010). *The case manager's handbook.* 4th edition. Sudbury, MA: Jones and Bartlett.

6. Dhand, S. (2015, June 1). Doctors: Be sure to thank the case managers. Medpage Today Professional. Retrieved April 10, 2016, from http://www.kevinmd.com/blog/2015/06/doctors-be-sure-to-thank-the-case-managers.html

Chapter 7: Deep Awareness, a Limitless Sky, and a Smile on My Face

1. Montessori, M., & Claremont, C. A. (1967). *The absorbent mind.* New York: Dell.

2. Oakley, B. (2014). *Mind for numbers: How to excel at math and science (even if you flunked algebra).* New York: Jeremy P. Tarcher/Penguin.

3. Ibid.

4. Ibid.

5. Myles, T. S. K. (2014). *The secret to peak productivity: A simple guide to reaching your personal best.* New York: American Management Association.

6. Dweck, C. (2016). Mindset for business & leadership. Mindset. Retrieved April 6, 2016, from http://mindsetonline.com/howmindsetaffects/businessleadership/index.html

7. Kaufman, J. (2014). *The first twenty hours: How to learn anything fast!* New York: Portfolio/Penguin.

8. Hill, N. (1937). *Think and grow rich: Teaching, for the first time, the famous Andrew Carnegie formula for money-making, based upon the thirteen proven steps to riches.* 2011 edition. Thinking, Inc., Media.

9. Duhigg, C. (2016). *Smarter, faster, better: The secrets of being productive in life and business.* New York: Penguin/Random House.

Chapter 8: Generating Vision for Leading

1. Cooper, B. B. (2013, Sept. 5). The 13 biggest failures from successful entrepreneurs and what they've learned from them. Buffer Social. Retrieved April 17, 2016, from https://blog.bufferapp.com/failure-entrepreneur-12-successful-entrepreneurs-tell-us-the-biggest-lessons-theyve-learned

2. Ibid.

3. Boyatzis, R. E., Goleman, D., and McKee, A. (2015). Primal leadership: The hidden driver of great performance. *On emotional intelligence.* Boston: Harvard Business School Press.

4. Ibid.

5. Ibid.

6. Ibid.

7. Heifetz, R. A., Grashow, A., & Linsky, M. (2009). *The practice of adaptive leadership: Tools and tactics for changing your organization and the world.* Boston: Harvard Business Press.

8. Boyatzis, R. E., Goleman, D., and McKee, A. (2015). Primal leadership: The hidden driver of great performance. *On emotional intelligence.* Boston: Harvard Business School Press.

9. Ibid.

10. Ibid.

11. Fryer, Bronwyn. (2013, Sept. 18). The rise of compassionate management (finally). *Harvard Business Review.* Retrieved April 10, 2016, from https://hbr.org/2013/09/the-rise-of-compassionate-management-finally

12. Boyatzis, R. E., Goleman, D., and McKee, A. (2015). Primal leadership: The hidden driver of great performance. *On emotional intelligence.* Boston: Harvard Business School Press.

13. Rindova, V. P., and Starbuck, William H. (1997). Ancient Chinese theories of control. *Journal of Management Inquiry,* 6, 144–159. Retrieved April 11, 2016, from http://pages.stern.nyu.edu/~wstarbuc/ChinCtrl.html

14. Oxfam International. (2016). Oxfam International: Our purpose and beliefs. Retrieved April 11, 2016, from https://www.oxfam.org/en/our-purpose-and-beliefs

15. Ikea Business Group. (2016). *Welcome inside our company.* Retrieved April 11, 2016, from http://www.ikea.com/ms/en_US/this-is-ikea/company-information/

16. Kouzes, J. and Posner, B. (2012). Vision statements from Fortune 500 companies. As cited in *Christianity Today.* Retrieved April 11, 2016, from http://www.preachingtoday.com/illustrations/2012/april/6040912.html

17. Ibid.

18. Ibid.

19. Under Armour. (2015). Vision. Retrieved April 11, 2016, from http://www.underarmour.jobs/why-choose-us/mission-values/

20. Kouzes, J. and Posner, B. (2012). Vision statements from Fortune 500 companies. As cited in *Christianity Today.* Retrieved April 11, 2016, from http://www.preachingtoday.com/illustrations/2012/april/6040912.html

21. Ibid.

22. Ibid.

23. Hill, N. (1937). *Think and grow rich: Teaching, for the first time, the famous Andrew Carnegie formula for money-making, based upon the thirteen proven steps to riches.* 2011 edition. Thinking, Inc., Media.

24. Facebook. (2016). Facebook's 5 core values. Retrieved April 11, 2016, from https://www.facebook.com/media/set/?set=a.1655178611435493.1073741828.1633466236940064&type=3

25. Ibid.

26. Hill, N. (1937). *Think and grow rich: Teaching, for the first time, the famous Andrew Carnegie formula for money-making, based upon the thirteen proven steps to riches.* 2011 edition. Thinking, Inc., Media.

27. Heifetz, R. A., Grashow, A., & Linsky, M. (2009). *The practice of adaptive leadership: Tools and tactics for changing your organization and the world.* Boston: Harvard Business Press.

28. Ibid.

29. Ibid.

30. Ibid.

Chapter 9: Assessing the Field

1. Ries, A., and Trout, J. (1993). *The 22 immutable laws of marketing.* New York: HarperCollins.

2. Bunger, J. D. (2008). Nurse entrepreneurs. *Nebraska Nursing News.* Retrieved June 24, 2016, from http://dhhs.ne.gov/publichealth/ Documents/NNfall2008.pdf

Chapter 10: Monitoring it All

1. Denning, S. (2011, July 8). The five big surprises about radical management. *Forbes.* Retrieved April 15, 2016, from http://www.forbes. com/sites/stevedenning/2011/07/08/the-five-big-surprises-of-radical-management/#3c6c66602c4d

2. Drucker, P. F. (2010). Managing oneself. *On managing yourself.* Boston: Harvard Business Review Press.

3. Huffington, A. (2014). *Thrive: The third metric to redefining success and creating a life of well-being, wisdom, and wonder.* New York: Harmony Books.

4. Drucker, P. F. (2010). Managing oneself. *On managing yourself.* Boston: Harvard Business Review Press.

5. Bradt, G. (2014, May 27). Trying to manage millennials? Give up and lead them instead. *Forbes.* Retrieved April 15, 2016, from http://www.forbes. com/sites/georgebradt/2014/05/27/trying-to-manage-millennials-give-up-and-lead-them-instead/#e95664411ba7

6. Pozin, I. (2014, April 17). 4 surprising truths about workplace productivity. *Forbes.* Retrieved April 15, 2016, from http://www.forbes.

com/sites/ilyapozin/2014/04/17/4-surprising-truths-about-workplace-productivity/#3c17836ce46e

7. Bradt, G. (2014, May 27). Trying to manage millennials? Give up and lead them instead. *Forbes.* Retrieved April 15, 2016, from http://www.forbes.com/sites/georgebradt/2014/05/27/trying-to-manage-millennials-give-up-and-lead-them-instead/#e95664411ba7

8. Concept Draw. (n.d.). SWOT analysis example. Concept Draw. Retrieved April 15, 2016, from http://www.conceptdraw.com/samples/resource/images/solutions/SWOT-analysis-instructional-sample.png

9. Taylor, N. F. (2016, April 1). SWOT analysis: What it is and when to use it. *Business News Daily.* Retrieved April 15, 2016, from http://www.businessnewsdaily.com/4245-swot-analysis.html

Chapter 11: Empowering the Most Engaged Players

1. Shontell, A. (2013, March 9). How Elon Musk hires: "It matters whether someone has a good heart." *Business Insider.* Retrieved April 15, 2016, from http://www.businessinsider.com/how-elon-musk-hires-it-matters-whether-someone-has-a-good-heart-2013-3

2. Cooper, B. B. (2013, Sept. 5). The 13 biggest failures from successful entrepreneurs and what they've learned from them. BufferSocial. Retrieved April 17, 2016, from https://blog.bufferapp.com/failure-entrepreneur-12-successful-entrepreneurs-tell-us-the-biggest-lessons-theyve-learned

3. Ibid.

4. Pink, D. (2009). *Drive: The surprising truth about what motivates us and why.* New York: Riverhead Books.

5. Ibid.

6. Ibid.

7. Bulygo, Zach. (2012). Entrepreneurial lessons from Mark Zuckerberg. Kissmetrics Blog. Retrieved April 17, 2016, from https://blog.kissmetrics.com/lessons-from-mark-zuckerberg/

8. Zetlin, M. How to build a culture of accountability. Inc. Retrieved April 17, 2016, from http://www.inc.com/minda-zetlin/how-to-build-a-stand-up-culture.html

9. Ibid.

10. Ibid.

11. Ibid.

12. Heifetz, R. A., Grashow, A., & Linsky, M. (2009). *The practice of adaptive leadership: Tools and tactics for changing your organization and the world.* Boston: Harvard Business Press.

13. Zetlin, M. How to build a culture of accountability. Inc. Retrieved April 17, 2016 from http://www.inc.com/minda-zetlin/how-to-build-a-stand-up-culture.html

14. Ibid.

15. MacMillan, A. (2011, Sept. 1). Insomnia costs U.S. $63 billion annually in lost productivity. CNN. Retrieved April 17, 2016, from http://www.cnn.com/2011/09/01/health/insomnia-cost-productivity/index.html

16. Bennett-Smith, M. (2012) Looking at cute animal pictures at work can make you more productive, study claims. *Huffington Post.* http://www.huffingtonpost.com/2012/10/01/looking-at-cute-animal-pictures-at-work-can-make-you-more-productive_n_1930135.html

17. Heifetz, R. A., Grashow, A., & Linsky, M. (2009). *The practice of adaptive leadership: Tools and tactics for changing your organization and the world.* Boston: Harvard Business Press.

APPENDIX A

PROFESSIONAL NURSING ORGANIZATIONS

- Academy of Medical-Surgical Nurses
- Academy of Neonatal Nursing
- Air & Surface Transport Nurses Association
- Alliance for Psychosocial Nursing
- American Academy of Ambulatory Care Nursing
- American Assembly for Men in Nursing
- American Assisted Living Nurses Association
- American Association of Bariatric Nurses
- American Association of Moderate Sedation Nurses
- American Academy of Nurse Assessment Coordinators
- American Association for the History of Nursing
- American Association of Bariatric Nurses
- American Association of Cardiovascular and Pulmonary Rehabilitation
- American Association of Colleges of Nursing
- American Association of Critical Care Nurses
- American Association of Diabetes Educators
- American Association of Heart Failure Nurses
- American Association of Legal Nurse Consultants
- American Association of Managed Care Nurses
- American Association of Neuroscience Nurses
- American Association of Nurse Anesthetists
- American Association of Nurse Attorneys
- American Association of Nurse Life Care Planners
- American Association of Nurse Practitioners
- American Association of Occupational Health Nurses
- American Association of Office Nurses
- American Association of Spinal Cord Injury Nurses

- American Burn Association
- American College Health Association
- American College of Healthcare Executives
- American College of Nurse-Midwives
- American College of Nurse Practitioners
- American Forensic Nurses
- American Heart Association: Council on Cardiovascular Nursing
- American Holistic Nurses Association
- American Long Term & Sub Acute Nurses Association
- American Medical Informatics Association/ Nursing Informatics Working Group
- American Medical Writers Association
- American Nephrology Nurses Association
- American Nurses Association
- American Nurses Association RN Action
- American Nursing Informatics Association
- American Organization of Nurse Executives
- American Psychiatric Nurses Association
- American Society for Metabolic and Bariatric Surgery
- American Society for Parenteral and Enteral Nutrition: Nurses Section
- American Society of Ophthalmic Registered Nurses
- American Society of Pain Management Nursing
- American Society of Perianesthesia Nurses
- American Society of Plastic Surgical Nurses
- American Society of Plastic & Reconstructive Surgical Nurses, Inc.
- American Thoracic Society: Nurses' Section
- Association for Applied Psychophysiology and Biofeedback
- Association for Professionals in Infection Control and Epidemiology, Inc.
- Association for Radiologic & Imaging Nursing
- Association of Camp Nurses
- Association of Child and Adolescent Psychiatric Nurse Division, International Society of Psychiatric-Mental Health Nurses
- Association of Community Health Nursing Educators
- Association of Operating Room Nurses
- Association of Nurses in AIDS Care

- Association of Pediatric Oncology Nurses
- Association of periOperative Registered Nurses
- Association of Rehabilitation Nurses
- Association of Women's Health, Obstetric and Neonatal Nurses
- Baromedical Nurses Association
- Case Management Society of America
- Chi Eta Phi Sorority, Inc.
- Childbirth and Postpartum Professional Association
- Commission on Graduates of Foreign Nursing Schools
- Dermatology Nurses' Association
- Developmental Disabilities Nurses Association
- Endocrine Nurses Society
- Emergency Care Connection
- Emergency Nurses Association
- Ethics & Compliance Officer Association
- Gerontological Advanced Practice Nurses Association
- Global Alliance of Urology Nurses
- Hospice Association of America
- Hospice and Palliative Nurses Association
- Infusion Nurses Society
- International Academy of Nurse Editors
- International Association of Forensic Nurses
- International Council of Nurses
- International Federation of Nurse Anesthetists
- International Nurses Society on Addictions
- International Nursing Association for Clinical Nursing Simulation
- International Organization of Multiple Sclerosis Nurses
- International Society of Nurses in Cancer Care
- International Society of Nurses in Genetics
- International Telenurse Association
- International Transplant Nurses Society
- National Academy of Dermatology Nurse Practitioners
- National Association for Home Care
- National Association of Clinical Nurse Specialists

- ▸ National Association of Directors of Nursing Administration in Long Term Care
- ▸ National Association of Geriatric Care Managers
- ▸ National Association of Hispanic Nurses
- ▸ National Association of Long Term Care Administrator Boards
- ▸ National Association of Neonatal Nurses
- ▸ National Association of Nurse Massage Therapists
- ▸ National Association of Nurse Practitioners in Women's Health
- ▸ National Association of Orthopedic Nurses
- ▸ National Association of Pediatric Nurse Practitioners
- ▸ National Association of Rural Health Clinics
- ▸ National Association of School Nurses
- ▸ National Association of School Nurses for the Deaf
- ▸ National Association of State School Nurse Consultants
- ▸ National Association of Travelling Nurses
- ▸ National Black Nurses Association, Inc.
- ▸ National Certification Board of Pediatric Nurse Practitioners and Nurses
- ▸ National Council of State Boards of Nursing
- ▸ National Federation for Specialty Nursing Organizations
- ▸ National Gerontological Nurses Association
- ▸ National Hospice and Palliative Care Organization
- ▸ National League for Nursing
- ▸ National League for Nursing Simulation
- ▸ National Organization of Nurse Practitioner Faculties
- ▸ National Society of Genetic Counselors
- ▸ National Student Nurses Association
- ▸ Navy Nurse Corps Association
- ▸ North American Nursing Diagnosis Association
- ▸ Nurse Practitioner Healthcare Foundation
- ▸ Nurse Practitioner Society of Dermatology Nurses' Association
- ▸ Nurses Christian Fellowship
- ▸ Nurses Organization of Veterans Affairs
- ▸ Nurses Without Borders
- ▸ Nursing Network on Violence Against Women International

- ▶ Oncology Nurses Society
- ▶ Pediatric Endocrinology Nursing Society
- ▶ Preventive Cardiovascular Nurses Association
- ▶ Respiratory Nursing Society
- ▶ Rheumatology Nurses Society
- ▶ Sigma Theta Tau, International Honor Society of Nursing
- ▶ Society for Endocrinology
- ▶ Society for Interventional Radiology
- ▶ Society for Vascular Nursing
- ▶ Society of Clinical Research Associates
- ▶ Society of Gastroenterology Nurses and Associates, Inc.
- ▶ Society of Otorhinolaryngology and Head/Neck Nurses
- ▶ Society of Pediatric Nurses
- ▶ Society of Urologic Nurses and Associates
- ▶ Space Nursing Society
- ▶ The Transcultural Nursing Society / College of Nursing Health
- ▶ Uniformed Nurse Practitioner Association
- ▶ World Home Care and Hospice Organization
- ▶ Wound. Ostomy, and Continence Nurses Society

ABOUT THE AUTHOR

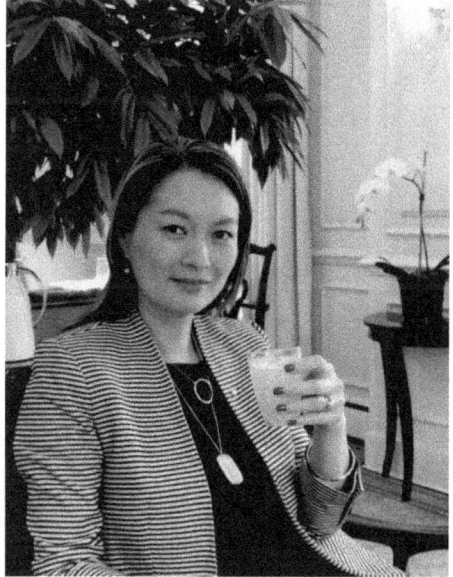

Lily Huang Carrier is a dynamic and successful nurse entrepreneur and business mentor. She worked as a medical-surgery nurse, built a thriving post-operative care business and hosted a television program to invite international entrepreneurs to help local businesses grow, which was broadcast across China.

Lily has been drawn to teaching and coaching all her life. She earned her Master of Arts in Education degree from Guangxi Normal University, where she also served on the faculty. Leaving behind her career, country, family, friends, and everything she knew that defined who she was, she embraced her visiting scholar opportunity and the challenge of staying in the United States.

With just two suitcases, she was able to build a new life. She earned her nursing degree from Michigan State University, worked as a critical care nurse in different settings, built a prosperous life plan elder law and business law practice with her husband, and founded her coaching and training company, Nursing Career Consultants.

Her entire life has been inspired by her ancestors. Her grandparents were successful business owners. Their struggles and wisdom, their entrepreneurial spirit, ancient stories, and powerful life example inspired her to build her own future, full of respect, freedom, and prosperity.

Lily would like to share with you all that she has acquired along the way, from the practical to the philosophical.

If you have a dream, and have the vision to believe in your dream, you can transform, and create the life you dreamed of.

—Lily H. Carrier

If you would like to share your story or feedback with Lily,
or would like to ask Lily questions, she would love to hear from you.
Please write to her at lily@NursingCareerConsultants.com

If you would like to know more about Lily's Nursing Business Success
Techniques, please obtain her FREE eBook at NCC website:
www.NursingCareerConsultants.com